OLD WINE IN NEW SKINS

OLD WINE IN NEW SKINS

Centering Prayer and Systems Theory

Paul David Lawson

Lantern Books • New York
A Division of Booklight Inc.

2001
Lantern Books
One Union Square West, Suite 201
New York, NY 10003

Printed in the United States of America

Library of Congress Cataloging-in-Publication Data

Lawson, Paul David
        Old wine in new skins : centering prayer and systems theory / Paul David Lawson
        p. cm.
        Includes bibliographical references.
        ISBN 1-930051-29-8
        1. Pastoral theology—Episcopal Church. 2. Church controversies—Episcopal Church. 3. Contemplation. 4. Systems theory. I. Title.

BX5965 L35 2001
253'.01'1—dc21

                                        2001038047

This book is dedicated to Bo, whose courage in facing his learning disabilities gave me the courage to face mine, and to Duffy who belled the cat. I would like to thank the following people: Carol Froom, who took care of all the details, Kathleen Dale, who introduced me to systems theory, Thomas Keating who taught me to listen to God, and Gail Graham and all the teachers at Mission High in San Francisco.

Table of Contents

Chapter 1 – Introduction

Assessment of Need

For five years I worked in the office of the Episcopal Bishop of the Diocese of Los Angeles as a member of his executive staff. While clergy deployment was not part of my duties, the topic of troubled congregations and clergy would often come up during senior staff meetings and in conversations with the bishop. At one time eighteen congregations, out of thirty-two vacancies in the Diocese of 150 congregations, were euphemistically classified as "unique." In other words, there were major problems with leadership transition in these eighteen congregations.

The eighteen congregations were classified as unique in spite of the fact that the diocese was reluctant to classify congregations, as classifications complicated filling clergy vacancies. That is not to say that problems were routinely swept under the rug; rather, without overwhelming evidence of a presenting problem, the Diocese assumed the congregation was in good shape. One congregation was represented to me as needing just a little more dynamic leadership, as the current minister was more interested in counseling rather than congregational ministry. Later, that minister would sign a confession admitting to eight instances of sexual misconduct with members and over thirty-six instances with prostitutes.[1] Before this position was filled, the Diocese began to uncover some of the problems; but the Diocese did not delay in filling the position, nor did it recommend an interim minister.[2] Years after being called, the new minister of this congregation was still uncovering severe problems with this church and attempting to work with those problems to bring about health and healing in the congregation.

There were two reasons, I believe, that the diocese sought to fill positions as quickly as possible. The first was the shortage of trained interim ministers and the belief that keeping trained interims on call was prohibitively expensive.[3] The second reason was the deeply held belief that the best way to fix a broken congregation was to find the right minister and get that minister in place as quickly as possible.

Placing responsibility for the solving of the problems of a community on the shoulders of one individual is a core belief of Western culture. This understanding of problem solving is ancient—Akhilleus and Odysseus in Homer's *Iliad* and *Odyssey* respectively present this image. More modern versions of this understanding are found in today's cinema in movies such as *High Noon* and *Rambo*. Unfortunately, what works in the plots of books and movies does not necessarily work in churches and synagogues. The fact that this is a program that does not work has not caused church administrative bodies to abandon it, the thought being that, after all, the right person just needs to be found. This is a theory that carries its own explanation for failure; that is, "We did not have the right person." Whether the theory works or doesn't, no outside explanation is necessary.

During the time I worked for the Diocese, it was not unusual to see clergy, after having been sent into troubled congregations, terminated after a year to eighteen months, or quitting or taking a disability retirement. Since the Episcopal Church has a plethora of clergy, there was never a shortage of people to send into the breach. Those who were unsuccessful were categorized as incompetent, and those who were successful were extolled as being paragons of virtue and worthy of advancement.

The View from Space
The view of congregations, when working for an adjudicatory body, is significantly different from the view held by individual churches and synagogues. It is perhaps analogous to the view from space as compared to the view standing at a particular spot on the Earth. On Earth, you see whatever is before you: mountains, plains, rivers, or oceans. Sometimes you can see two or more of these features together when the visibility is really good. But, from space, you can see it all, the whole Earth with all of its topographical features and all its constituent parts forming an interrelated whole. The view from a diocese or synod office is much like the view from space. It is an opportunity to see patterns and features that are not visible from an individual congregation.

The view was staggering. From the Diocese one could see a constant running balance of between seven and eighteen congregations that were in various types of upheaval; six priests at one time were under suspension; two priests were in jail; and congregations that, just fifteen years previously, had thousands of members were struggling with fewer than one hundred. Not all of this could be blamed on shifting demographics or dangerous liberal policies driving away membership.

Anomalies
While working at the Diocese, I noticed several anomalies in clergy placement. The first was that prior performance was not an indicator of success when placing clergy in troubled churches. Clergy who had done well in past calls went down in flames at the same rate as did mediocre clergy. Clergy who in the past had no aberrant behaviors on their record were suddenly assaulting lay

leaders, while others were developing a fondness for barnyard animals.

The second anomaly was that, in many cases, there was no direct cause for clergy resignations or terminations. Often in such cases, the behavior of the congregation or clergy was no different in the period leading up to their termination than it had been over the previous year in which no termination had taken place, nor could any behavioral change be projected over the upcoming year. Why then, had the separation taken place at that time and not some other time if there was no precipitating cause?

The third anomaly was the inability of dioceses to see that sending clergy into troubled congregations was much like the fabled charge of the Light Brigade.

G. Lloyd Rediger in his book, *Clergy Killers*, states that a minister is fired every six minutes in the United States and twenty-five percent of all ministers have been fired at least once. Yet minister after minister is sent in to work in a troubled congregation without a clear understanding of the work to be done or the risks involved.[4] There was a heavy price to be paid in terms of lost vocations, yet no alternatives to "business as usual" were ever discussed. My attempts to open this discussion, both formally and informally, were sometimes met with resistance, but more often were just ignored; and I was told to stay in my own area of expertise. There was a lack of openness to change.

In the summer of 1993, a new Canon to the Ordinary was appointed, The Reverend Canon Anne Sutherland Howard. After one of her first staff meetings, I continued to make a point about clergy placement and the way troubled congregations were handled by the diocese long after the discussion had been closed. She suggested that perhaps I might like to take a church that was experiencing difficulties and try out my theories of church leadership. It seemed to me a good idea at the time, and I decided to take her up on her offer. I believed that if I had a working model of the theory I had been talking about, it would be easier for others to understand. I further believed that, if I was successful, the work I was doing could provide a blueprint for work in congregations with chronic problems. Neither of those beliefs proved to be accurate. This book is a result of the work that I did at the diocese and then at the congregational level.

Thesis

The purpose of this book is to offer an alternative way of looking at leadership in congregations. In the past, leadership has often involved hierarchical models, a mechanistic worldview, a fix-it-or-replace-it understanding of church management and clergy deployment. The alternative includes understanding the congregation as a whole and concentrating on the relationships within the congregation rather than concentrating on the individual parts that make up a congregation. Natural systems theory provides a framework and a method for such an understanding.

But understanding alone is not enough to effect change in leadership. Centering prayer provides a powerful tool to help transform this understanding into a reality. Centering prayer can lower overall reactivity which, in turn, lowers anxiety in the congregational system, fosters responsibility, encourages openness, and provides the security that is necessary to promote self-differentiation.

The thesis of this book is that a combination of systems theory and centering prayer provides a way to apprehend the functioning of congregations that is closer to a modern understanding of the way the world works than are current methods of management and leadership. Applied together, these two disciplines, one new, the other old, provide a more effective and productive way of understanding and working with leadership at the congregational level.

The Argument

Congregations have been increasingly experiencing major problems in the area of leadership over the last decade. There has been a growing awareness of reactivity within congregations. Reactivity can be behaviors by both clergy and congregations that are based on emotional feelings rather than thought-based actions. These behaviors can range from personal attacks and aggressive behavior to total withdrawal from the community. These actions are a non-thought based attempt to displace anxiety. This increased reactivity has resulted in a decline in membership; loss of revenue; cutbacks in programming; early involuntary separations; and, in some cases, even the closing of churches within many denominations and different religions. This is not a phenomenon that is restricted to the Christian faith. Whether this increase in reactivity is caused by the failure of medieval church structures in a twenty-first century world or just an overall increase in societal anxiety is immaterial; the effects being felt in the congregations are the same.

In an attempt to solve the problems created by this increased reactivity and anxiety, the church has without a lot of success turned outside itself for help to a variety of psychological and managerial models. Each year brings new methods to solve these problems taught in books and through seminars that have little effect on the overall functioning of the congregations.

The road to success in healing a congregation and lessening reactivity begins with understanding the causes of the reactivity. Natural systems theory provides an effective method to do this. The road to healing begins with an understanding of anxiety and its causes that produce the reactivity within the congregation. Once anxiety is understood as a normal part of life, working constructively to bind anxiety within the congregation becomes an attainable goal. Understanding what triggers anxiety, and learning to discriminate between the causes and symptoms of anxiety, can lead to healing.

Differentiation, which is a process of self-regulation and self-organization, can help individual leaders regulate their own responses to anxiety. Their responses are ultimately the only things they can regulate, but self-regulation of anxiety response by the leadership can lead to self-regulation on the part of the congregation.

Natural systems theory provides new and more accurate ways of thinking about congregational emotional problems. It provides a way of understanding congregational relationships and the forces that animate life. Natural systems theory helps leaders to understand the processes of mutual interdependence within the congregational system.

Centering prayer provides the method that helps individuals and congregations change patterns of behavior that are generational. It is divine therapy. As motivations and behavior change, the reactivity within a congregation lessens, individuals take more personal responsibility, and more time can be devoted to ministry and less to corporate regulation of the anxiety of a few individuals. The end result of all of this is congregations equipped for ministry instead of conflict.

Method and Resources
The focus of this book is three areas. The first is observation and reflection on myself as a congregational leader in relation to the theory and practice of centering prayer and natural systems theory, and the effects the implementation and integration of these theories had on my practice of congregational leadership. The second is my experience with two congregations that I have served that have had a history of conflict and severe dysfunctional behavior resulting in the abrupt termination of the pastoral relationship with their clergy and a concomitant drop in membership and revenue. The third is my experience and

observations at the diocesan staff level, as a senior staff member of a large diocese overseeing one hundred and fifty congregations.

This is more than just an experiential book. Added to my experience is a combination of theory and reflection. There are two primary theories put forth in the book. One is the theory of centering prayer and the other is that of natural systems. Both of these theories become actualized in practice. The process, I believe, takes place in the following order: experience or practice followed by an infusion of theory; reflection on the theory; and practice resulting in a new practice and experience. At this point, the process begins again. The following is a record of this process.

* * *

After I returned from overseas service as a missionary, I attended graduate school, since the average re-employment time for returning church missionaries was eighteen months and the church paid six months salary as a resettlement package. While I was at the university, a nearby congregation imploded on Christmas Eve. The rector either resigned or was fired after the evening service. The bishop asked me if I would take over for a few weeks. Ultimately this temporary assignment stretched into five years. It was only a matter of weeks before it was clear that oral prayer and petition were not adequate for me in this hot bed of reactivity. Someone suggested that I contact a Roman Catholic abbot, Thomas Keating, who was beginning to reformulate and repackage a traditional form of Christian prayer. I attended an introductory workshop in Austin, Texas, and began the practice of centering prayer.

After several months of practice, I went to St. Benedict's monastery at Snowmass, Colorado, for more intensive practice and experience of centering prayer. For ten days I did as much as six hours of contemplation each day, interspersed with periods of *Lectio Divina*, liturgies and lectures by Keating. This experience resulted in a change in my understanding of life and also brought about a change in my lifestyle. My awakening to the drives for power, control, security, affection, and esteem in human life, and the afflicting emotions that accompany them, began a process that led me to understand my own behavior and the behavior of others. The theory of centering prayer led to practice of prayer which, in turn, led to new understandings, which led to different practice.

The practice of centering prayer led to a lowering of my overall reactivity to the chaos around me. This allowed for more objectivity in my decision-making process. Centering prayer not only lowered my stress level, but I noticed actual changes in my physiological responses to threat, aggression, and challenge. Through the unloading of the unconscious, or purgation, as part of the prayer process, I was able to separate my own reactivity and personal issues from those of the congregation in which I served. This resulted in a clearer and more objective leadership process. The security that I felt from a deeper relationship with God contributed to a willingness to take risks and be more open in my leadership of the congregation.

I was able to replicate these same effects that I experienced personally in the congregation through the formation of centering prayer groups. At one time, I had over sixty people practicing centering prayer in a congregation of 220. The overall reactivity of the congregation went down and the overall tolerance for differences went up.

Shortly after I began to practice centering prayer, I read in an article in *SPICE*, a newsletter for clergy spouses, about Edwin Friedman's book, *Generation to Generation*.[5] My wife and I began to apply natural systems theory to our own immediate family and, later, to examine our relationships and positions in our families of origin. Through the lens of natural systems theory, patterns of behavior in our lives and our families became clear. Recognizing those patterns became the first step toward changing behavior. Following the same pattern that I did with centering prayer, after first applying natural systems theory to my own life, I began to apply the theory in my congregational work. This theory had a significant impact on my understanding of leadership. Having once subscribed to the Tiglath-pileser or "Pulu" school of management,[6] and handing out eighteen unsolicited letters of transfer to a neighboring congregation for my most troublesome members, I now took a less reactive approach, recognizing my role in the congregational relationship system. I now understood that the individuals involved were only performing functional roles that would be performed by others if they were not available. Health came in understanding the mutuality of the relationship system and in working with the process rather than focusing on individual members or events. On the individual level, it meant teaching and practicing that leadership was defined as taking responsibility only for one's own actions and reactions, while being in relationships with all others.

I later applied the pattern established in this congregation to other congregations and in my work with the diocese. In looking at congregations as a whole, patterns of behavior emerged that could be traced back through the history of the congregation, much as an individual's behavior could be traced back to their family of origin.

Now I see that problems can be seen more objectively as systemic rather than the fault of any one individual or even any group of individuals. Natural systems theory can be used to understand the relationships and workings of a congregation, and to work at beginning the process of healing, utilizing the concepts of differentiation, triangles, generational transmission, projection process, functional position and emotional cut-off. Particularly important is the understanding of the role of the leader as one who maintains emotional clarity and acts rationally and encourages the same behavior in others. Centering prayer then is used to lessen emotional reactivity and to purge and heal those deep hurts that cause emotional reactivity. Centering prayer also helps promote a value structure that is conducive to unconditional acceptance of others.

Together, natural systems theory and centering prayer provide the method and the tools to effect change in congregations today. They are compatible in promoting nonreactive leadership; they encourage responsibility and choice, provide emotional clarity, and encourage trust and openness. Natural systems theory provides a blueprint for change. The fruits of centering prayer enable people to amend life and to accept others unconditionally as you are accepted and loved by God unconditionally. These theories complement each other in that they help actualize and bring into reality the interior goals of each.

There were two major periods of transition during the time I was working with these theories and putting them into practice. The first was the transition from a church to diocesan level assignment. This provided an opportunity for me to get a wider view of congregational ministry. It also allowed me to put into practice some of the changes I had made in my understanding upon reflection on my experience. Usually, I was confined to giving advice and suggestions; but for one six-month period I was assigned to an American Baptist Church as a co-pastor. This allowed me to field test some of my new understandings.

The second period of transition was that from a supervisory capacity on staff to congregational ministry. While I had several years to develop the theory, I knew that the practice would be very difficult. I built in some safeguards to this transitional period. One was a five-year, no termination contract; another was money set aside by the congregation to hire a consultant to help me monitor my reactivity and objectivity. I correctly perceived that it was impossible for me, going into this particular highly reactive situation, to retain my objectivity and nonreactive state in the face of constant verbal attack.

Finally, I applied for and received a grant to form a group composed of clergy who worked in congregations that were considered highly reactive. The group consisted of twelve clergy from a variety of congregations throughout the diocese. The congregations were diverse in size, ethnicity, economic status, and viability. Each congregation had a history of problems often stretching back over generations. Some of these problems had involved inappropriate clerical behavior, acting out by church members, or involuntary separations. The approach of this group was to assume that the clergy would ultimately be drawn into the established cycles of conflict unless they could maintain a low level of personal anxiety and reactivity. Through monitoring and regulating the clergy leader's anxiety, the level of anxiety and reactivity in the congregation could also be regulated. The leader's refusal to participate in cycles of conflict would gradually lead to change. The group experienced a ninety percent success rate as opposed to the normal thirty or forty percent success rate previously experienced when working with conflicted congregations.[7] Success was measured by increases in giving and membership, continued employment by the clergy, a decrease in identifiable reactive incidents, and anecdotal reports.

Definitions and Terms

The two major terms used in this book are natural systems theory and centering prayer. Both are terms that are often used imprecisely outside their own fields. Natural systems theory is a term that is often confused with systems thinking and used interchangeably with systems theory. Natural systems theory is an understanding of human nature based on evolutionary biological science.

Proponents of natural systems theory argue that it is not based on concepts of general systems theory. They say that general systems theory was influenced by man-made systems such as steam, electricity, rocket science, and computers. Mathematical concepts were then applied to biology and other behavioral and social sciences.[8] The "natural" in natural systems refers to the observation that families occur in nature and are not a construct of the human mind. They are, instead, a part of the evolutionary system. Humans don't create family systems, they discover them. This fact sets natural systems theory apart from other family therapy theories such as Milan, Brief, or Structural. Murray Bowen believed that human emotional functioning extended beyond the human constructs of such theories in their relatedness to all life. Bowen also believed that in order to understand the behavior of an individual, it was not enough to consider only the individual. The individual's relationship to the system needed to be an integral part of the equation.[9]

This understanding is not necessarily the understanding of all those who work with natural systems theory. Peter Steinke says that natural systems theory is a way of conceptualizing reality.[10] Bowen and Michael Kerr would disagree with this and say that natural systems theory exists in reality.

Centering prayer is a term that came to be applied to a method of prayer taught in a workshop by Basil Pennington to a group of religious superiors under the sponsorship of the Major Superiors of Men.[11] The members of Pennington's order had used the term centering prayer in reference to the book *The Cloud of Unknowing* and to the exercise of prayer that is described therein. Pennington suggests that the usage may have come about because Thomas Merton, who was a member of their order, often spoke of going to one's center to pray. Those who practice this type of prayer suggest beginning the prayer by choosing one word such as "God" or "love,"[12] then repeating the word until it disappears. Pennington felt that this was a sign of a movement toward the center, so he called it centering prayer.[13] This was a term that Thomas Merton had used in his writings.

The method itself was developed as an attempt to move people toward contemplation. Originally, this had been the function of *Lectio Divina* but over time, each part of *Lectio Divina* — *meditatio*, *oratio*, and *contemplatio*[14] — had become compartmentalized and an end in itself rather than preparation for a deeper experience.[15] Another consideration was that in the modern world outside the monastery, not everyone had the time to devote to *Lectio*. Centering prayer offered a method to move directly into contemplation without the large blocks of time that *Lectio* requires. In its modern form centering prayer is an ideal form of spirituality that can lessen the normal anxiety that exists in society today and particularly within congregations.

This project begins with a look at the role that anxiety plays in congregational ministry today. We live in a society where many of our institutions are in a state of change. This creates uncertainty and a variety of pressures focused on congregations and their ministers. In this situation, more is expected, and people have less tolerance for error.

Chapter 2 – The Pastor and the Church Anxiety Machine

The Situation

In the last few years, an increasing number of congregations have become unstable, resulting in the separation of their clergy or even, in some extreme cases, the dissolution of the church itself.

Several causes have been advanced for this phenomenon.[1] Viewing this situation from a natural systems perspective, one of the causes for this instability can be traced to uncontrolled anxiety on the part of both clergy and laity. Though anxiety is a widely experienced phenomenon, conceptually it is not very well understood among clergy and laity. This lack of understanding often leads to severe problems within congregations between the clergy and the laity. Typical questions needing attention include: What is anxiety? What triggers anxiety? How is anxiety displaced? How is anxiety managed? Is there a way to decrease the overall anxiety found in churches today? What role do differentiation and responsibility play in this process? This book attempts to answer these questions and, in doing so, shows the role that anxiety plays in the increase of congregational instability. Sometimes storytelling is the best way to understand a formal concept.

Death World Trilogy

Harry Harrison, in his science fiction novels *Death World Trilogy*, envisions a planet where all the living creatures are connected through mental telepathy and act together in times of stress for their survival.[2] Colonists come to the planet and inadvertently kill some animals. The planet then classifies the colonists as a natural disaster and the animals band together and begin to mutate. The entire ecosystem of the planet has only one goal: to rid itself of the invaders. The invaders, on the other hand, see themselves as just trying to eke out a living. The colonists develop fantastic training methods that begin with infants in the cradle; eventually they become the deadliest killers in the galaxy. Unfortunately, the planet also evolves into the deadliest planet in the galaxy. The colonists continue to lose ground, no matter how well trained they are, and are eventually all but driven off the planet.

Hope for the future comes when, with the help of an outsider, they discover that the planet is reacting to their violence and reaction. The ultimate cure is non-reaction; and, with this, the potential for harmony on Death World is established. Many of the original colonists are not able to adjust to this new situation and have to leave the planet since they continue to react even though the threat is gone.

While this story is a science fiction novel written over thirty years ago, the landscape of the planet that is described in the novel looks a lot like the landscape of a late twentieth century congregation. The next section of this project will take a closer look at the topography of the congregations and their similarity to the world of science fiction.

Death Church Trilogy

"*Death Church 1*": *Midwestern Plains*. Following a seventeen-year incumbent, who took the parish from a small mission to a medium-size congregation, the new minister was having a spot of trouble. His predecessor was a dynamic preacher and a good liturgist. These are not the new minister's gifts. Unknown to him, he was the search committee's fourth choice, the first three having turned the committee down.

Soon after the minister began, the liturgy committee began meeting with him to go over the service in detail, pointing out exactly where he had gone wrong during celebration of the service. The service was dissected from hymns to prayers, and, in each area, fault was found with the new minister's performance. Each sentence during these meetings began with, "Father Jim used to do it this way" or "Father Jim said the liturgy should always be done this way."

During services, one member of the church would sit in the front row. After the sermon started, he would get up and walk outside until the sermon was over, and then he would return. If the sermon went on too long, the organist would begin playing the next hymn when the minister paused to breathe. The minister, for his part, began making plans to install stained glass windows with pictures of the Blessed Virgin Mary in them in this very reformation-oriented church. After less than two years, the pastor quit or was fired (there are two versions of this story) on Christmas Eve.

"Death Church 2": Mountains of Appalachia. After a popular five-year incumbent moved to a larger church, this congregation called an interim minister. The interim minister was placed by the bishop, who was of a different political persuasion than the congregation and its previous clergy. The church leaders had been convinced by the bishop that they had to select one of the clergy that he sent to them, all of whom were politically incompatible with the congregation.

One year into the contract, the bishop offered to make the minister permanent. The congregation and the minister accepted.

Within a few months, every plan the minister suggested was rejected by the church governing body. His stewardship plan was not approved, and a lay commission was formed to develop a new one. The plan that was finally approved was almost identical to the one the minister had submitted. The minister had several small children, who played in his office before and after the service. The church council came to the minister and told him that he needed to keep his children out of his office as this was not conducive to Sunday worship. The minister submitted his resignation after a year. When a consultant was sent in to help facilitate the termination, he asked the congregation what the problem was. They replied that the minister showed no leadership. In looking at the figures, the consultant saw that attendance was up, as was pledging; and the Sunday School was growing. When confronted with this apparently successful record, the congregation said it was accomplished in spite of the minister's lack of leadership.

"Death Church 3": Baltimore. A new minister was chosen the week before the church's annual meeting, and at this meeting the people who chose the minister were turned out of office. They left the church, leaving the minister with a hostile governing body. After the first few months in office, while doing his taxes, the minister discovered he had been underpaid. He asked the church leaders to make an adjustment in his paycheck. They told him to get a lawyer. At a staff meeting during his first year at this church, a lay leader threw open his door and said, "Pete, get out here now." Pete replied, " I am in the middle of a meeting." The church leader responded, "Pete! Out! Now!" The pastor slunk out of his office past his staff. The church leader said, "I have found another example of your massive incompetence. The Council board minutes have been filed without their plastic sheet protectors." In a few months, the minister submitted his resignation.

Congregational Placement Problems

There are several different theories for the recent increases in the number of "Death Churches." In an article in *Leaven*, a clergy association newsletter, G. Lloyd Rediger writes, "This time I am describing the more vicious game in which a pastor is targeted for destruction, and the congregation is seriously damaged by the fallout."[3] He goes on to describe this game as one of "clergy killing." The cause behind it, he says, is "evil." He describes the people involved in these activities as "paranoid, antisocial, borderline, histrionic, narcissistic, and even passive aggressive."[4] He goes on to say that "they may have developed a perverse, voyeuristic, and vindictive taste for the suffering of their targeted victims."[5] This is a point of view that has found much support among the clergy, as it absolves them of any responsibility for the relationship system.

Dioceses or adjudicatory bodies on the other hand, are more restrained. They see the problem as one of need for more training or a different kind of clergy placement system. The *au courant* model is the clergy "lend/lease" program. In this program, the clergy and the church try each other out for a year and a half; if it is good for both of them, then, after another year and a half, the minister is given a permanent contract. If either party is dissatisfied with the relationship, a new search is begun. At last, serial monogamy has been institutionalized by the church. Dioceses defend this program as being a "no fault" way of avoiding bad clergy placement. The underlying presupposition is that church problems are solved by good clergy placement, regardless of the settings into which the clergy are placed. Again, this is a solution where the focus and responsibility are placed on the clergy. You now have both the laity and the oversight body both holding the clergy responsible for the entire relationship system. Simply stated, the equation is Good Clergy equals Good Churches. Congregations and oversight bodies are both looking for one good person to fix everything. They believe that success will come for the congregation when that savior is found.

Another popular solution is a modified systems approach. If we look at our own family-of-origin issues and the congregational family-of-origin issues, we can see where clergy and the congregation have become enablers of each other's points of conflict. If we identify and eliminate these points of conflict, then everything will be all right. In other words, we can identify the true problem and solve it.

None of these solutions takes seriously the congregational system itself. Each of these understandings of the congregational ecosystem identifies the problem as being with one part of that system that needs replacing or fixing, much like a faulty part on a car that won't run, rather than the result of the system's functioning as a whole. This comes from a very mechanistic worldview.

Understanding Anxiety

Saint Paul says, "And I will show you a still more excellent way (1 Cor. 12:31). A more excellent way of viewing congregations might be as a potential anxiety machine. In order to understand this model, it is important to understand the meaning of the word *anxiety* as used in natural systems theory. Kerr and Bowen in their book *Family Evaluation* define anxiety as the response of an organism to a real or imagined threat.[6] This reaction includes increased emotional activity in response to environmental threats. It makes no difference whether the threats are real or imagined; the response that is triggered is the same, much as the ecosystem is in Harry Harrison's book. One side begins the violence, the other side responds with violence, and a chain reaction is begun that continues forever. Kerr and Bowen describe this activity as taking place along a continuum that ranges from behavioral frenzy to behavioral paralysis.

One congregation used to call an emergency meeting of either the governing body or the congregation as a whole whenever the level of anxiety began to rise. After being in place for two months, their new interim minister left the state on a four-day church-related trip. When he returned home, he discovered that an emergency meeting had been called for that evening to discuss the church property that may have been in danger from rising flood waters. The church was rallied, experts were called in, and no flood danger was found to exist. The flurry of activity had taken place over the several day period that covered the new minister's absence, thereby displacing the anxiety that his absence created.

Anxiety is Normal

An important key to understanding anxiety in the congregational setting is to understand that anxiety is normal and natural. Anxiety occurs, not only in human beings but also in mammals, fish, birds, and, alas, congregations. The question becomes not whether you have anxiety, but how you manage it, whether you are in a community of baboons, human beings, or in a congregation. Edwin Friedman suggests in an article in the *Handbook of Family Therapy* that "[anxiety] is less something that is unnatural (that is, neurotic) than the exaggeration of a basic rhythm of life."[7]

Acute and Chronic Anxiety

Kerr and Bowen describe two types of anxiety, acute and chronic.[8] Acute anxiety is anxiety that occurs in response to a real threat; by its nature, it is time-limited, for there is, in fact, a bear in the woods. You can do something about that, such as run or climb a tree. If you climb a tree the problem is solved. If you get eaten you no longer care. Chronic anxiety occurs in response to imagined threats and, as such, it is not time-limited. There might be a bear in the woods; it might know my name; it might be headed for my house today, tomorrow, or the next day. Since the threat is not real there is no solution and therefore no way to relieve the anxiety. People can adapt to acute anxiety fairly easily. One can see the bear, and climb a tree. Chronic anxiety is much more difficult to adapt to as the possibilities are limited only by a person's imagination.

There is no one cause for chronic anxiety since there is, in fact, no bear in the woods. Chronic anxiety is most easily visualized as a process, not an event, the result of a variety of actions. Once started, it takes on a life of its own, independent of any direct stimuli, say Kerr and Bowen. What generates chronic anxiety is a change in a relationship system. Once change takes place, then the reactivity around the change takes on a life of its own. Reaction to the reaction becomes the primary generator of anxiety. You have the beginnings of the parish anxiety machine. No further cause is necessary, no further stimulus is required. Perpetual motion has been discovered.

Zombies

The Cranberries, a popular rock group from Ireland, had a recent number one record album called *No Need to Argue*. The lead track on this album is entitled "Zombie." The lyrics to the refrain go, "In your head they are fighting....Zombie, What's in your head? They are fighting."[9] This song alludes to the fighting in Belfast that has been going on for so long that the response is automatic. Killing begets killing. So, too, is the automatic response of chronic anxiety. Once started, like the killings in Belfast, it can go on for generations claiming victim after victim with no immediate cause other than the reaction to a reaction. "What's in your head, Zombie?"

Causes for Anxiety

In a congregational setting, the original cause for anxiety could be the retirement of a minister, the arrival of a new music minister, the death of a prominent church member, or just about any event that changes the relationships significantly within the congregation. In "Death Church 1," the founding father of the congregation left. This deeply upset the relationship system within the church. The new minister arrived, and the problems began as the system tried to readjust itself.

Edwin Friedman in his book *Generation to Generation* makes a helpful distinction between process and content. Process is emotional and is about relationships. Content is about specific events and is often symptomatic.[10] Clergy inadvertently step into the anxiety "bear trap" at this exact point. Unfortunately, a minister who tries to work with the content rather than the process is frequently doomed to failure and winds up wondering what happened. Individual content problems can be solved; but, unless dealt with, the process issues will only resurface as different content problems.

For example, in "Death Church 2," the first content issue was the stewardship campaign. Once that issue was resolved, the children playing in the office on Sundays became the new content issue. In this particular church, there were over twenty of these content issues before the minister finally chose to leave. Friedman lists over sixty possible content issues when the focus is on the clergy.[11]

Anxiety, then, is always with us. It may be personal anxiety from our lives and our relationships, such as family problems or work-related problems or problems relating to the family of origin; or it may be systemic anxiety from the relationships within our church. The latter can be relationships between the minister and congregation; between the minister and the staff; among the staff, such as between the Christian education director and the choirmaster; or, finally, among members of the congregation itself. The anxiety can be chronic anxiety in reaction to an imagined or future threat (the church might burn down or the minister might leave); or it can be acute anxiety caused by a real and immediate threat (such as concern that the church can't pay salaries this month because no one has pledged).

Anxiety Triggers

As if all these sources of anxiety weren't enough there are the additional sources of anxiety that are inherent in all animal life. In an article in the journal *Family Systems* entitled "Chronic Anxiety, the Adrenocortical Response, and Differentiation," James E. Jones writes about what affects an individual's response within a relationship system. Jones cites Robert Sapolsky's studies of baboons and identifies three triggers of anxiety response. The first is being in a subordinate position in a dominance hierarchy. The second is being in a group that lacks a stable dominance hierarchy. The last is being separated from one's important relationship partners.[12]

The first two of these triggers can be found in most church organizations, and the last in church organizations where the leader has formed close and/or long term relationships with church members. The first case, being subordinate in a dominance hierarchy, appears to be a trigger well suited for church organizations. Churches are filled with archbishops, elders, priests, lectors, deans, bishops, choirmasters, deacons, prophets, lay leaders, and Christian education directors. The language of these titles lets you know that in most religious organizations you have a hierarchy. Struggles for dominance can take place between ministers and oversight bodies, ministers and laity, between lay departments and among clerical staff. The possible combinations are almost limitless.

In the second case, groups lacking a stable hierarchy, the church is also a fertile field for anxiety. In addition to the struggles for dominance listed in the first case, which can cause hierarchical instability, there are also other sources of instability. One possible source is an ever-evolving society where roles are not as clear as they once were, thereby leading to struggles for dominance. Another possible source for instability is the increased mobility of church leaders, both lay and ordained. In many religious groups, clergy stay fewer than ten years. Moves after two or three years are not uncommon. This instability can lead to anxiety.

The last case that Jones mentions is that of being separated from important relationship partners. This too can occur in churches when the church leaders form strong attachments to the members of the congregation and then move, quit, or are terminated.

It can be seen from the above examples that church organizations can become, to quote James Taylor's popular song "Steamroller," "a churn'n urn of burning funk." To recapitulate, in any church organization there is potential for anxiety from both acute and chronic sources. This anxiety can be both real and imagined, from relationships among individual members or from church system relationships. The anxiety from these relationships can be from the present relationships or from families of origin.

All of these are sources for original anxiety in a church structure. This anxiety is only the beginning, for the reaction to the initial anxiety then becomes the source for new and intensified anxiety.

In the example of "Death Church 1," we saw the minister respond to the anxiety of an unstable hierarchy caused by the departure of a seventeen-year incumbent. This was expressed by the church in the content issue of criticism of his worship and preaching style, and by the minister in choosing to raise the anxiety level in the congregation by injecting the content issue of the reserved sacrament. His reaction only served to heighten the anxiety and continue the struggle.

Finally, another cause of anxiety within churches is that of secrets. Friedman writes in *Generation to Generation* that secrets "exacerbate other pathological processes unrelated to the content of the particular secret, because secrets generally function to keep anxiety at higher energy levels."[13] In addition, Friedman says that secrets block communication, divide families, create false companionship and false divisions, and distort perceptions. When congregational problems are kept secret, solutions to the problems cannot be found. Often secrets produce behavior that on the surface looks odd. If you don't know the secret, you don't know why someone or some congregation acts the way he, she, or it does. Secrets also marginalize individuals and produce triangles. When two people withhold information from or information about a third person that person becomes an outsider. Secret meetings create an "in" group and an "out" group. Secrets subvert open process and clarity.

In one congregation there had been a history of child abuse which no one ever talked about. As a result, when new people came into the congregation, they had a vague, uncomfortable feeling that there was something that they didn't know. Any issue involving children invoked an aggressive response from long-time members. Some new members of the congregation wanted a nursery, but the long time members refused to vote the funds. Some new members wanted a children's choir and the minister refused to even consider the proposal. The new members went away feeling unheard and rejected. In each of these cases secrets led to feelings of disappointment and rejection for reasons that were not related to current issues.

In the field of geography, there is the conundrum known as the Mediterranean Puzzle. Water flows into the Mediterranean from both the Black Sea and the Atlantic Ocean. There are also numerous rivers which flow into the Mediterranean, but there appears to be no outflow. The question is, where does the water go, since it does not overflow and flood Europe? Count Luigi Marsili, in 1679, discovered that while the surface water flowed in, there was an undercurrent that flowed out because of a difference in water density. This is also the case with the emotional current in congregations. Emotional density that doesn't overflow will lead to deep undercurrents.

An example of this phenomenon is a church that founded a day school on its property. As years went by, the school grew until it was larger than the church, and certainly richer. Soon religion was not taught in the day school, and even an opening prayer was discontinued. The school paid for many of the church expenses. When a new minister arrived at the church, he suggested that a school chaplain be hired and religious education be taught, not an unreasonable request for a church school. Within days, a civil war broke out; within weeks, the minister was fired; and, within months, over one quarter of the membership left the church.

Managing Anxiety

In the article "Chronic Anxiety: The Adrenocortical Response and Differentiation," Jones writes that the baboons manage the anxiety level in their societies by provoking a winnable fight. Dominants attack subordinates when their anxiety level is high. Subordinates are subject, then, not only to the acute anxiety of a real threat, but also to the chronic anxiety of imagined and possible threat. Thus, dominants are able to shift their anxiety to subordinates. Hierarchical church organization is ideally suited for this method of anxiety shifting.

Kerr and Bowen suggest that anxiety can be managed through the formation of relationships. Baboons' struggle for dominance is certainly one way of forming relationships and managing anxiety. Kerr and Bowen state that, as the anxiety in a given situation increases, so does the pressure for togetherness; anxiety management can be found in efforts to insure that groups act and think alike. The greater the anxiety, the greater the pressure to act and think alike. The reaction to this pressure for togetherness is the need for isolation and distance. Caught between these two forces, people become more irritable and less tolerant. Kerr and Bowen also identify other ways of managing anxiety, including drugs, alcohol, overworking, overeating, and acting out sexual fantasies, to name just a few. Anxiety can also be played out in chronic anger.

All of these are ways of managing anxiety in a group and in relationships. But they can also increase anxiety for others in the relationships. Almost anything people can do in a group can be a way of managing anxiety. Unfortunately, these ways can also increase anxiety for others in the group or the level of group anxiety as a whole. How, then, can we manage anxiety in church organizations without beating up on each other, taking to drugs or alcohol, overeating, overworking, or acting out sexual fantasies? The key lies in the natural systems concept of differentiation, which is a process of self-regulation, self-organization, and self-definition.

Differentiation
The key to understanding differentiation is to understand it not as an event or something to be grasped by the beholder but as a process that is life-long, continual, ongoing, and neverending. It is truly our own neverending story, always a work in progress; it is never finished for as long as we live.

Friedman talks about differentiation as clearheadedness in his article, "Bowen Theory and Therapy." It is, he says, "an emotional concept not a cerebral one." He goes on to say that this concept has its origin in the idea that cells have no identity until they have separated from their originator. At the same time, a cell must remain in contact with other cells or it has no purpose. One frog cell does not a frog make. Friedman says that differentiation is being one's own person while being in contact with others. It is the capacity of being a self with a minimum of reactivity to others. Emotional reaction becomes a choice rather than an automatic response to systemic stimuli. It is being emotionally clear when making judgments and decisions. This is, says Friedman, a way of focusing on strength rather than on pathology. It is the ultimate call to personal responsibility for one's self and one's actions and reactions.

When differentiation takes place in the leadership of a church organization, the entire organization benefits by a lowered level of reactivity. Differentiation offers the possibility of a response to church organizational anxiety that does not involve a transference of anxiety to another, or inappropriate, behavior.

Differentiation creates the space between individuals that is needed for healthy functioning. It cuts down on the amount of automatic emotional reactivity to acute and chronic anxiety. It also cuts down on the amount of reactivity to reactivity. It encourages independence and allows for differences. How different things might have been if the minister in "Death Church 1" could have functioned independently and not raised the level of anxiety in the content struggle, but rather taken the opportunity to point out the natural anxiety in the loss of a seventeen-year leader who had grown close to many of the church members! Understanding differentiation might provide a way for church leaders to work with anxiety within a church organization, rather than leaving that organization. The following case study illustrates what can happen to a congregation when the anxiety within the congregation is not managed through the process of differentiation but is left to grow unchecked at great cost to both individuals and the congregation itself.

Death Church: The Ultimate Conflict

A non-denominational church in a suburb of a large southern city called a new minister after what turned out to be a six-year interim following the thirty-year incumbency of the founder. This church was a medium-size church of about 1,000 members; it had been active in starting a free clinic under the founder. This church was politically moderate in most areas, but it had a strong Right to Life group. After the founder, a very active pastor, strong leader, and tireless home visitor had retired, the church called a business-oriented minister from the North to follow him, after a two-month interim. The founding pastor made an effort to stay away from the church, attending another church in a nearby community; but his presence was felt, for he still lived in the area.

The new pastor never quite "fit." He was a Yankee, he did not seem very friendly, and he never stopped to chat or invite anyone over. He was, however, a good businessman, and while church enrollment began to shrink with the retirement of the founding pastor and the end of the 1950s, the money from the investments that the new pastor made kept the revenue about the same. There were also some major problems during his six-year tenure. He had barely settled in the community when a clinic in town began performing abortions. While the church's clinic did not do abortions, it did counsel women as to their choices. In the minds of many of the townspeople, the two clinics were confused. Pickets began to show up during church services and the church was burglarized and vandalized. More people left the church, and pressure mounted to close the church's free clinic. The church divided into pro-life and pro-choice factions and the membership declined. Eventually the church was forced to close its clinic, hire guards for its services, and sell its minister's home and buy another one in a community farther away from the church. Membership and attendance continued to fall.

After several years passed, the old pastor came back to sit in the congregation and things appeared to quiet down. In the fifth year of the new pastor, the Sunday School teacher resigned and admitted to having had an abortion. The church immediately exploded. Pro-life and pro-choice groups chose sides and the battle was joined. The minister was accused of hiring a staff that lacked moral fiber. The minister's and staff's private lives were the subject of some talk and investigation. The next year, the minister resigned after a bout of health problems. The church took two years this time to call a new minister. During this time of an interim pastorate, the lay members of the church were able to make decisions for the first time in thirty-eight years, and they came to like doing so.

They finally called a new minister; in a stroke of daring, they called a woman. For the first six months, everything was fine. While attendance did not grow by leaps and bounds, it did show a small increase, which was better than the losses incurred over the previous ten years. But there were beginning signs of strain: while the previous incumbent was never mentioned and the past troubles never even obliquely referred to, every sentence in conversation began with, "The founding Pastor said...." Coffee hour chat mostly centered around events from the early 1950s. Reverend Joline, the current pastor, began to get worried and feel anxious. She embarked on projects to redesign the Fellowship Hall and began to change the Order of Worship. She began to hire more staff, which put a strain on the budget, but enabled her to do more of the day-to-day operations of the church from her office and depend less and less on volunteer workers. Soon, even the smallest detail of church life was planned from Rev. Joline's office. She gathered a small group of church members around her and began meeting only with them. She even redesigned the church office so her office was no longer accessible through the main reception area. Church members now had two secretaries to get past in order to see her.

After the end of the first year of her ministry at this church, the community in which her church was located began to plan a city-wide pro-choice demonstration. Although she took no part in the organization, Rev. Joline asked her assistant to help some church members who did plan to take part. The church began to react around this issue and groups began to form supporting or opposing the pastor. While she did not take a public role, Rev. Joline did craft an announcement for the church bulletin, published under the name of her assistant, announcing a downtown rally for free speech and the American way. The church exploded again. "Isn't this really an abortion rally?" said some.

The assistant was forced to apologize for the announcement he did not write, and he later resigned. Members of the congregation formed into active pro-choice and pro-life groups; anonymous letters were sent to the church leadership from both sides. Then rumors began to surface in the congregation that Rev. Joline herself, in her youth, had had an abortion. Sometimes she broke down during congregational meetings and would sob, "No one understands me." A few months later she took a one-month leave of absence. When she returned, she said that she felt like a new person, but soon she had stopped sleeping and within a month resigned. Church enrollment continued to decline.

This was a church with a very high degree of reactivity which managed to lose half its congregation, and three ministers; all left the active ministry, all in an eight-year span. When the founding minister retired, there was a loss of stability in the dominance hierarchy and the relationship system. There was also a loss of a significant relationship, since, for many in the church, the founding pastor was the only one they had ever known and the only pastor whom their children had ever known. The new pastor began to react to this reactivity and to close himself off from the congregation. A series of external events increased the anxiety to intolerable levels, and he left the ministry. Rev. Joline, who came in at this point, was forced to bear the brunt of ten years of anxiety caused by unsettled relationships, external factors, secrets, a struggle for dominance, and just about every possible anxiety factor. She ended up bearing the anxiety of the whole church's system of relationships, developed over a decade, in addition to some personal issues. As one person, she was not able to bear the weight of everyone's personal and corporate anxiety. There was too much anxiety in this church for any one person to be able to displace.

In all of these Death Church examples, the relationship between minister and church is severed, not for any direct cause, but because of an increase in the overall level of anxiety within the congregational system. None of these ministers ran off with the church secretary, left town with the collection plate, or preached heresy; yet, at some point, their contractual relationships with the church were severed. There was a feeling on the part of either laity or clergy, or both, that "enough was enough." The "enough" was an intolerable level of anxiety within the system that was then displaced by the dissolution of the pastoral relationship.

In such a situation there is no single cause, so the congregation cannot just tell the minister, "You'll be fine if you just don't move the candlesticks." The way to end this rash of Death Churches is to be aware that the cause of dissolution is a process, not an event. Once the process has been recognized, identified, and understood, then other means to displace anxiety need to be developed. What is called for in the Death Church is specialized pastoral care for the system that involves specific steps toward healing and wholeness.

Beginning Steps Toward a Healthy Church

The road to success for this congregation will begin when their leadership is able to start the process of self-differentiation. The first step in this process is to *separate the content issues from the emotional process of the church anxiety machine.* In "Death Church 2," there were over twenty separate content issues ranging from

stewardship to children and, if the minister had stayed, there would
have been twenty more. The process issue was how the minister
came to be at the church. The fact was that the Bishop had
imposed him upon the congregation and he was a minister that the
congregation would not have chosen for themselves. Unless the
relationship among the minister, congregational leadership, and
Bishop were addressed, content issues would keep coming up. Since
that issue was never addressed, the situation reached a point where
the minister left.

The second step toward self-differentiation will occur when *the
church leaders can understand the sources of anxiety within their church
community*. Until ministers and lay leaders can sit down together
and discuss relational causes of anxiety, that anxiety will continue
to be a problem. In "Death Church 3," the church leaders were
never able to deal with the way in which a new minister had been
chosen by the outgoing leadership. Until that relational issue
among the old and new leaders and the new minister was settled,
there would never be peace. In this case too, the minister
ultimately left.

The third step will occur when *the leadership can take
responsibility for their own actions and not react automatically to
emotional stimuli*. When a person's children are being attacked, as in
"Death Church 2," it is hard to remain calm and not react. But
reaction only leads to more reaction and keeps the process going.
Ultimately, both ministers and clergy can only take responsibility
for their own actions. If you decide to let your children play in the
office, then you must live with that decision. If you decide to call
an interim minister, then you must live with that decision. If
someone does not like your decision, then that is their problem,
not yours.

The fourth step will occur when *the self-differentiated leadership
can begin to explain all of this to the congregation as a whole. Emotional
systems thrive in darkness*. The church leadership, both lay and

clergy, need to be able to explain process to people so they understand what is happening to them. The situation in "Death Church 1" might have changed if the minister had been able to say to the congregation that he knew he didn't preach like their old pastor and he understood they missed the old pastor, and that was all right. He could have expressed his hope that they would not take that grief out on him. The new minister could have perhaps helped the congregation express their grief in more constructive ways.

Through the practice of these four steps, the level of reactivity should decrease overall, although there will be some increase in localized disturbances. These should subside if the leadership can stay the course and continue the process of differentiation.

Conclusion

Churches are not doomed to become or continue to be "Death Churches." The church leadership needs to begin consciously and constructively to address anxiety as a process within the church. Anxiety is a natural part of being human, but there are choices in dealing with it. Anxiety needs to be understood. Process needs to be separated from content. Emotional triggers need also to be understood, and the resulting anxiety needs to be constructively managed. This can be accomplished through non-reactivity to automatic triggers and differentiation of self, first among the leadership and then among the church membership. Death Churches, like the original Death World, can have the possibility of hope for the future.

Following these steps is only a beginning. Creating a healthy church environment requires a complete reorganization of the way that the leadership of churches and congregations is understood. Leadership for the next century requires an understanding of more than the constituent parts; it requires, in addition, an understanding of the relationships among those parts. But neither all the understanding in the world nor all the correct practice will necessarily bring about a healthy congregation. The next step toward a healthy congregation is to look at natural systems theory and the ways in which the theory can be useful when applied in a congregational setting.

Chapter 3 – Natural Systems Theory

New Ways of Thinking

It is a commonplace now to hear that the world is just too big. Our countries and cities have become too large to be governed effectively. The invention of computers and the information superhighway have provided us with more information than we can possibly understand or digest. The world is just changing too fast. Things are just too complex. Many of the problems in organizations and congregations have been attributed to size, density, and the rate of change.

Searching for effective ideas for leadership, it is possible to find programs based on everything from war (Sun Tzu's *The Art of War*) to jazz (*Leadership Jazz*). They all have one thing in common: none of them works very well. Each year, a new batch of solutions is imposed on organizations and replaces the previous year's offerings. The bargain tables of bookstores are full. Perhaps, though, the problem is that our organizations were designed and created in a Newtonian world, but we live in a quantum age. Recent discoveries in science have led to new ways of perceiving the world. Some of the new discoveries include the interconnection of all living things, nonlinear thinking, and the separation of process from content.

Social institutions and organizations have drawn their *Weltanschauung* from science; the current worldview used by organizations is from the seventeenth century, but we live and work at the beginning of the twenty-first century. What this means practically is that we try to manage by breaking things into parts, and we believe that things are influenced by a direct exertion of force against an object or by one person against another.[1] We behave as if we live in a cause and effect universe. Margaret Wheatley, in her book *Leadership and the New Science*, calls this a mechanistic worldview, a world which is understood as if it were a clock with a pendulum swinging back and forth with regularity.[2] Everything in our lives is organized to fit this understanding. This is a world filled with limits, boundaries and direct causes. Twentiethicentury science posited a different world. In the physical sciences, it is a quantum world in which relationships are all that there is to reality. In the biological sciences, it is a world that is directly connected from the cellular level to the human level, from cell systems to human family systems.[3]

How human beings apprehend the world, and what they think about the world they apprehend, has changed radically throughout recorded history. Some scientists would have us believe that this change has been an orderly progression, a march of progress through recorded history. Human beings understood one thing, and then, as more facts were assembled, that understanding gradually changed to a true understanding of reality. But, in fact, this has not been the case at all. Instead, the history of science tells us that humans have believed one thing and then, seemingly overnight, changed to the opposite view. Instead of a gradual progression, through a building up of facts through the scientific method, a reversal of belief happens through a flash of insight. A flat world becomes round; a world a few thousand years old becomes billions of years old; the Earth that is the center of the universe becomes just another planet; particles become waves, and tables that appear solid contain more space than matter.

What is true of the physical sciences is also true of the biological sciences. Humans, viewed as distinct individuals different from other animals, become just another part of the food chain, products of evolution. Darwin's theory of evolution proposed that all living things were connected to each other by relationships and that all living things were mutually dependent upon each other.[4]

There are implications for churches and congregations in this way of viewing the world. Churches and congregations today are products of the past. The organizational structure is feudal, the church schools and their curricula are based on the Industrial Revolution's training methods for factory workers, and the buildings and worship services are products of nineteenth-century Europe. The church could survive all of this, except that when the church tries to change, it applies the same outmoded viewpoint. The church attempts to change and fix parts and replace individuals. Successful change and leadership will come when the church views the world as it is and makes changes that are more in keeping with modern understandings of reality. Natural systems theory provides one possibility for examining leadership in congregations that is in keeping with recent discoveries in the physical and biological sciences.

Natural Systems Theory—1

Natural systems theory is first and foremost a theory about nature. Edwin Friedman writes, "Bowen theory is not fundamentally about families, but about life."[5] Natural systems theory is more than just another family therapy. It is more than a tool to fix things. Michael Kerr writes, "Bowen theory defies conventional categorization. It is more than a psychological theory; it is not an outgrowth of general systems theory; it is more than the basis of a form of family therapy; and it has potential applications in the fields as diverse as medicine, biology, anthropology, law, sociology, and organizational management."[6]

Natural systems theory does not treat human beings as a special case in nature. Rather, natural systems theory posits that the same emotional forces and patterns of behavior at work in other species apply to humans equally.

Biological Connections

Natural systems theory is a theory about all life, because it is a biologically based theory rather than a construct of the human mind. The emotional processes that are at work in humans can be examined in life forms. Anxiety, for example, can be found and studied in marine snails. It seems that snails can become chronically anxious if they don't know when they are to receive an electric shock. If they get a consistent warning, then they are able to calm down between shocks. If they receive no warning, then they are always physiologically ready to be shocked. This is similar to humans worrying about what is going to go wrong next.[7] Michael Kerr says that what this study demonstrates is that more is needed than just making an effort to be less anxious. People need to feel that they can handle whatever difficulty they might face. Uncertainty breeds reactivity. Anticipating that something bad might happen creates physiological change, which is a physical component of anxiety.[8]

Michael Kerr recounts a study of Fortis Finches by Peter and Rosemary Grant that can tell us something about how the environment affects behavior.[9] In the study of Geospizafortis (a type of finch found in the Galapagos), cycles of drought and rain brought changes in both the physical characteristics and behavior of these birds. During a time of drought, the birds stopped pairing up to mate and concentrated on staying alive. During the next year and a half, many of the birds died and no mating took place. When it finally began to rain again, the birds began to pair up. The females did not pair up at random, but rather chose the strongest males with which to mate. There were other changes in the breeding patterns of the finch as well. Kerr describes the birds as engaging in a copulatory frenzy. A graduate student, Lisa Gibbs, is quoted, "In the steamy rains more and more birds were turning bigamous or polygamous...one female finch went through four males, one after the other."[10] The question of teenage pregnancy arose among the finches. The finches normally don't breed until they are two years old, but after the drought some bred as early as three months, behavior that had never before been recorded.

The behavior that was described was not particularly adaptive since, when the next drought occurred, bird death was everywhere. The increased breeding rate was not part of the process of species survival but an automatic response to anxiety created by a changing environment. What was described was an emotional response to a changing and anxiety-producing environment. What is meant by emotion in this description is more than just a record of feeling. A feeling is thought-based and reflective, while an emotion is the automatic response of an organism to its environment.[11] This response may be transmitted among others in the system, thereby affecting their behavior. This particular environment, drought and rain, produced changes in the finches' behavior, in their organization, and even in their physical makeup.

In a congregational situation with humans, observers would have difficulty examining behavior and changes without making moral and emotional judgments that might say more about the person observing than the process observed. It is possible for us to be dispassionate about finches, but we are not so dispassionate about ourselves. The finch study helps to illustrate the impact that the environment can have on emotional systems and organizations. The source of this impact is often lost in feelings and judgments about certain behavior. In working with congregations, emotional clarity is to be prized. **Ministry Tip:** It is helpful to remember that observation is fact, while motivation is fiction.[12] To put this another way, what we observe is a physical reality, but what we believe to be someone's motivation is our own mental construct, the reality of which may exist only in our minds. What people believe to be another's motivation tells us more about the person making the observation than it does about the process, person, or behavior observed.

James E. Jones writes about physiological responses and anxiety. Jones says that a high level of glucocorticoids is one way of carrying anxiety.[13] A high level of glucocorticoids helps an organism adapt and meet a threat, but this same high level over a longer period of time produces physical consequences that include hypertension, ulcers, diabetes, and other illnesses. It may also influence the interpretation of events around the organism. For example, a fight response might occur where no challenge was intended.

In studies of baboons, among the triggers found for this fight or flight response in the baboons' relationship system were an unsettled hierarchy, being a subordinate in a dominance hierarchy, and being separated from the relationship system itself.[14] All three of these causes for triggering anxiety are also found in congregational systems. Chronic anxiety and its physiological changes may cause an inaccurate interpretation of events, interpreting threats and challenges where none are intended, or producing threats and challenges where none are needed.

Nonlinear Thinking

Nonlinear thinking considers the relationship among the parts of a whole and the influence that they have on each other. In linear thinking, A causes B; in nonlinear thinking, A and B influence each other.[15] Even to say A, B, and C cause D is still linear thinking, as each is considered an independent actor acting as a lone agent, though, at the same time, they each contribute to cause

D. Nonlinear thinking holds that A and B and C and D all influence and have effects on each other. Friedman writes, "Each part of the system (including the effect itself...) is connected to, or can have its own effect upon, every other part."[16] To illustrate this understanding, Friedman uses the game of football. Only the most casual observer of the game believes that when the quarterback is sacked it is solely his fault, or when a pass is completed the quarterback alone did a great job. In both cases, blockers block, decoys decoy, throwers throw, and catchers catch. Coaches and assistants had to design plays and counter plays. For a pass to be caught or a quarterback to be sacked, there were literally hundreds of events that needed to influence each other in order for plays to be successes or failures.

This new way of thinking emphasizes the whole rather than any individual part, and the parts can only be considered in their relationships with the whole. It is a way of thinking that concentrates on structure rather than symptoms, and on the way a part functions within a system rather than on the part itself. It is a way of thinking that emphasizes process over content.[17]

Process and Content

This new way of thinking also emphasizes the examination of process rather than content. This is one of the most helpful distinctions for congregational ministry that Friedman makes. Often in congregational ministries, the minister gets caught working with content when the issue is process. The content may be the minister's sermons, the minister's children, church parking, or any one of thousands of content issues. The problem is that, when one of these content issues is solved, another content issue takes its place in a seemingly endless progression. Individual problems may be solved, but the overall anxiety level remains the same because the underlying process that caused the problems was not addressed.

Michael Kerr writes that the Greeks, beginning with Democritus, used system thinking when they made the distinction between the process of nature and the content of nature. The process is "a continuous series of actions or changes that result in a given set of circumstances or phenomena....Content refers to the circumstances or phenomena out of the context of those actions or changes."[18] Unfortunately, systems thinking was then ignored for the next two thousand years, says Kerr.

The distinction between process and content is in some ways similar to Thomas Aquinas' distinction between substance and accident. Substance is that which exists in itself; accident is that which can only exist in substance.[19] Process exists in nature and, while relationships change, the process of being in relationship does not change. It is a constant of life. Human beings exist in relationship to God, nature, and other human beings, not as isolated entities. Who or what humans are in relationship with may change, but the fact that they exist in relationship will not change. A person's pattern of relationship is set in their nuclear family, and it is a pattern that is continued throughout their adult life and adult relationships. **Ministry Tip:** Relationships are learned at home. Content constantly changes and only takes meaning as part of the process. Since content constantly changes within a relationship system, more lasting changes can come about by working with the relationship systems themselves rather than the ever-changing content. For example, a person who watched one of their parents relate to another through emotional outbursts may continue this pattern when they reach adulthood. They may continue this pattern not only in their family but also at work or in the congregation. In order to work successfully with this person a pastor needs to understand this person's pattern of behavior.

In congregations, many of the struggles that take place are not about the content or the issues of the struggle but instead are about a person's place within the relationship system. In one congregation the young mothers in the nursery wanted to replace the adult-size toilets with child-size toilets. The building and grounds committee, which was made up primarily of people over sixty, refused to authorize the work. They said, "We didn't need special toilets for our kids" and "This church has been here a hundred years without special toilets and it will be here a hundred more without them." This is the same committee that had, a year earlier, rejected baby-changing tables in the men's room as being unmanly. This congregation had recently experienced a rapid spurt of growth, attracting people with small children. The children were now coming to services, making noise, and their parents were taking up parking spaces and wanting to do things differently. The older generation was uncomfortable with the new members. The new members wanted to have some sign that their concerns were being addressed by the establishment. The content shifted and changed between changing tables and toilets, but the real issue or process was the relationship between the generations. The question was, "Is there a place for me in this congregation?"

This was a question not only for the new people, but also for the members of long standing. At the same time that the buildings and grounds committee was rejecting the request from the nursery for small toilets, some of their members came to the minister and asked if it would be possible to have a reception for the donor of a new rug for the library. The minister, who was not paying close attention to the "whole," told the members that they would have to submit a request to the congregation's governing body, as that was the process that was now being followed in the church. The governing body told them they would have to make their request in person since the budget process had been completed. After a month, the money was granted. Several weeks later, the minister noticed that some minor repairs were needed in the church. The minister mentioned to the chairperson of the buildings and grounds committee that some work needed to be done in the church. The chair responded that the minister needed to present the request in writing. As of this date, no children's toilets have been installed, no repairs to the church have been made, but a reception for a long-time donor has been held.

In this case, the minister might have had more success if he had agreed to hold the reception and told the older members of the church that the minister would go to the governing body of the church and make the request for funds. The issue was never about receptions. The question was, "Do you love me?"

In working with congregations, it is helpful to note that content can act as a warning that there are some process issues that need to be addressed, or it may simply reveal the constant anxiety that is part of life. The anxiety issues and the content will normally disappear over time unless the leaders react to keep them going. When working with a congregation, the focus needs to be on the process rather than a particular problem. The leadership should seek to understand the process itself, its role in the process, the place of anxiety in the process, and how that anxiety affected the way both lay and clergy functioned in the congregational situation. **Ministry Tip:** It is almost never content; it is usually process. Success comes in working with the process not the content.

Natural Systems Theory—2

One of the seminal modern thinkers in the field of psychiatry and family therapy was Murray Bowen. Bowen began looking at relationships in families in a new way. Much of the work he did is now the basis for what is called family therapy. Bowen broke with the psychiatric thinking of the time in saying that, in understanding human beings, more is involved than just the individual's psychology. In order to understand human beings, their relationships with all life must be considered. Further, the relationship system in which an individual lives must be part of the understanding of that individual.[20] The basic assumption is that a human being is part of an emotional process, as is all of life. It is evolutionary in nature and goes back to cell life. All people today function in, and are still part of, that emotional system.

Bowen began working with these ideas in the area of schizophrenia. He treated the whole family rather than just the individual. His theory was that schizophrenia was a three-generational evolutionary process. Bowen did his work in the Menninger Clinic and later at the National Institute of Mental Health. At the National Institute, Bowen had entire families live on a hospital ward. It was here that he began to develop his theoretical concepts that became the basis for family systems theory. Bowen then moved to Georgetown University where he expanded his theory to include not just the nuclear family, but also the extended family. He proposed an alternative to cutting off the patient from the family for treatment. The alternative was to understand the patient's role in the family system. It was a system to be based on observable facts about the family system, not the feelings produced by that system. Bowen observed how the family members related to each other rather than how they felt about each other.

Under the leadership of Bowen, the Georgetown Center continued to expand the theory. While the basic concepts and understandings had their origins in the work of Bowen, others made contributions. Michael Kerr continued to develop an understanding of the emotional system as something that occurred in nature, the effects of which were felt from the simplest cell life to the most complicated human beings. Edwin Friedman, a rabbi, used this theory in working with churches, synagogues, and other organizations which functioned in many ways like a family and were part of an emotional system. Underlying these expansions were still the basic concepts of natural systems theory. These same concepts are an integral part of working with natural systems theory in the congregation today.

The Theoretical Concepts

Natural systems theory is composed of a number of interlocking concepts that form the building blocks of the theory. Natural systems theory is a theory of the "whole."[21] It is a theory that seeks to examine the relationship among the parts of the whole. The parts mutually influence one another, and this relationship of influence can be understood and studied as a whole. This whole, in turn, influences and regulates the parts.[22] Kerr writes that the problem with talking about the whole is that, unless you can say how the parts are influenced, you are then talking philosophy and not science. The theoretical concepts are a way of talking about how the parts are influenced by each other and by the whole.

The theoretical concepts also provide a way in which to understand the theory itself. Understanding "wholes" is a new way of thinking. It is more difficult for people to grasp concepts than to understand the individual parts. Darwin wrote about this difficulty in understanding his theory of evolution. The human mind has a problem simultaneously understanding all the steps in a gradual process.[23] In the theory of evolution there are billions of factors that mutually influence each other over millions of years. The human mind appears to be more comfortable with a single-cause or a multiple-cause understanding, rather than an understanding that involves a system of interdependence and mutual influence over an extended period of time. Our understandings are based on a mechanistic view of the world. Our understandings of this new way of thinking are limited by our disciplinary and conceptual boundaries.[24] The theoretical concepts provide a form in which to apply and understand systems theory.

The Emotional System

Some of the major authors who write about natural systems theory begin with a different theoretical concept. Some begin with the concept of differentiation of self, some with the concept of triangles. Michael Kerr begins with the emotional system. It is the first concept for him because of two factors: first, that it provides a new understanding of the human family; secondly, that it provides a behavioral link between humans and other animals.[25] Friedman says that the emotional system highlights what is important about families, such as levels of differentiation, triangles, and anxiety, rather than culture, gender, or environment.[27] This is another way of talking about process and content.

Differentiation, triangles, and anxiety are processes that remain basic and constant. Culture, gender, and environment are content and constantly shifting. For example, being Swedish at the beginning of the twenty-first century is hardly seen as an important factor in church or congregational management. Being Swedish is an accident of birth and not considered a major factor in church governance in the same way that being Black, Hispanic, or Asian is seen to impinge on church organization. Yet, only a few hundred years ago the wall that Wall Street was named after was built to keep the Swedes out of the good part of town, while Philadelphia built "Old Swede Church" so the Swedes could have their separate, but equal, facility. At the current rate of population growth in California, it will be only a few years until the White or Anglo population will be a minority. What cultural issues will surface then?

Because the emotional system is biological and not a human construct, differentiation, triangles, and anxiety are still the crucial factors they were two hundred years ago, and as crucial as they will be two hundred years from now. The emotional system is all of an organism's mechanisms for driving and guiding it through life.[27] Some of these responses are automatic, while others include responses that are partially learned. These can include thoughts, feelings, metabolic states, drives for food, sex, rest and migration, and generational processes. These are, for the most part, automatic and instinctual. The individual is shaped by this system and, in turn, shapes the system. In our language, we have terms for this kind of functioning: we talk about "gut reactions" or "intuition." How often is it said, "I just have a feeling?" This feeling is the result of a complicated emotional process. Peter Steinke writes, "Whenever humans interact, emotional and physical processes happen. Human interactions are full of information and are mutually influencing."[28]

In working with congregations, an understanding of the emotional system can make these processes visible and understandable. This visibility, in turn, can lessen the automatic functioning of the system and offer a congregation opportunities for choices. The automatic functioning of the emotional process is always present and influencing events—even when you cannot see it—and needs to be taken into account when working with a congregation. **Ministry Tip:** Emotional process is like gravity: you can't see it, but it is always there.

Anxiety: An Animating Principle of Life[29]

Anxiety is a natural part of life. Anxiety is movement. Anxiety is, perhaps, the dance of life. Life without anxiety is static and stationary. There is no change without anxiety. Everything remains the same without anxiety. There is no impetus for change without anxiety. Daniel Papero says that anxiety is the arousal of an organism in response to a threat that can be either real or imagined.[30] Arousal is the movement from a state of rest to a state of action. But anxiety is more than just movement, it is a dance. It is a dance of individuality and togetherness.

Michael Kerr calls individuality and togetherness the two counterbalancing life forces.[31] Individuality is the force that is reflected in the desire to think, act, and feel for oneself. Togetherness is the force that is reflected in the desire to be dependent, connected, and an indistinct entity.[32] It is the tension between these two forces that creates a balance in the relationship system. It is this movement or dance that is the relationship process. This process animates and drives a congregation toward either balance or imbalance in relationship, toward stability or chaos. Focusing on this relationship process is key to working successfully with a troubled congregation. When the relationship system is in balance, then the anxiety level is lowered and the ability to adapt and respond to change is higher.

Staying focused on the relationship system is hard to do. The human mind appears to want to slide from a systemic understanding to an understanding of the particular. One of the ways in which the mind does this is to ask the question "why?". In asking why Mr. Doe behaves the way he does, the focus is taken off the relationship system and placed on an individual behavior or person. In congregational settings, often it is heard said, "Mr. Doe is upset because...." The "because" could be because he is angry, offended, or disappointed in some action or series of actions that the church or its leaders took or failed to take. It could also be some issue or stand that the church or its leadership has taken. Once again, the focus has been diverted to the individual rather than held on the process. All of this assumes that the cause of the behavior lies *within* the person rather than as a result of the interaction of the forces of individuality and togetherness.[33] All interactions reflect this process: the need to withdraw or to come closer, the need to run away or to pursue.

The balance between the need for individuality and the need for togetherness in the relationship process is in a state of continual flux. What determines where the balance is placed between individuality and togetherness is the amount of energy that is put into the relationship. If a lot of energy is put into a relationship, then a person is more bound to the relationship and less able to function on their own and the balance is more on the side of togetherness. If less energy is put into the relationship, then a person is able to function more autonomously and is able to be more flexible and adaptable to change and the balance is more on the side of individuality.

It is important to remember that relationships are not only with other persons, but also with ideas, institutions, or even committees. Every church has members who believe they are the church, the altar guild, or the choir. A perceived injury or threat to any of these groups is taken as a threat to that person. The hostility engendered in some church debates can be better understood if seen in this light—that is, as threats to the very existence of a person who has placed an inordinate amount of energy into a relationship with a church idea or group. If enough energy is put into the relationship, then the boundaries between self and other disintegrate.

This process of differentiation between self and other can also be observed at the cellular level. Friedman writes about a study in 1970 involving organisms from species that had not evolved immune systems. It was known that creatures from the same species will fuse on contact if they don't have an immune system,[34] thus blurring the distinction between the self and non-self of these organisms. Keeping cellular boundaries is why organs are rejected in transplantation: the body sees the transplanted organ as not part of itself.

In the experiment, the smaller cell began to disintegrate as it moved closer to the larger cell. The larger cell did nothing to cause this disintegration, and within twenty-four hours the smaller cell had lost all of its properties of organization. The smaller cell had lost the ability to discriminate between itself and a non-self. The lesson to be learned from this, says Friedman, is that auto-destruction was induced by moving a creature closer to a member of its own species.[35] **Ministry Tip:** Be connected; not engulfed.

The less energy that is put into a relationship and the more energy that is kept to use in a person's own functioning, the more differentiated a self is said to be.[36] The more differentiated a self is, the less anxiety is felt in trying to conform to group positions, and the more flexibility a person has in adapting to change.

This has important implications for congregational ministry. It is especially important to consider where ministers choose to put their time. Too often, ministers spend their time asking "why" something happens, rather than looking at the totality of the relationship system. Heated arguments over choir robes that end in members leaving the church are often more about individuality and togetherness than about the actual robes. How often do people within a congregational system alternate between choosing to die over the color of a robe, then leaving the church if the choice doesn't suit them? They are alternating between losing the boundaries of self and creating the boundaries of self. At first they lose self to the choir or church entity by over identifying with a particular issue, then they regain self by withdrawing altogether and leaving the church.

Ministers who worry too much about the color of the robes, or whether church member X is happy with the color, are directing their focus on areas that in the long run will not be productive. In addition, ministers and leaders need to examine their own relationship systems and their own process of differentiation. How much of a minister's self is invested in the church, its committees, its programs, and its positions? **Ministry Tip:** Don't care about the results. The minister can work with a number of different outcomes in any given situation and does not need to be emotionally invested in any one particular result. Success ought not to be measured by winning or losing in any particular situation, but rather by the ability the minister has to work with any outcome. How much of the anxiety in church congregations is caused by loss of self and lack of differentiation, which in turn reduce flexibility and adaptation to change? The goal of church leaders should be achieving relationship balance within the system of a congregation, rather than solving individual problems.

Differentiation

Michael Kerr writes, "Differentiation describes the process by which individuality and togetherness are managed by a person and within a relationship system."[37] Friedman says, "Differentiation means the capacity to become one-self out of one's self with a minimum of reactivity to the positions or reactivity of others."[38] The key words in these definitions are "process" and "become." Both words suggest and depict that movement as differentiation is not a static concept or a thing achieved but rather a process, a becoming, a direction of movement. It is the process of balancing and managing the life forces that creates energy and anxiety. It is a natural process originating in cell life.

Murray Bowen described this process as a scale, which he says is the cornerstone of his theory. The term "scale," he says, conveys the idea that people are different and that this difference can be measured.[39] The scale ranges from low to high levels of differentiation. Those people who have achieved the highest levels of differentiation are those whose actions and decisions are mostly thought-based. Michael Kerr calls this the ability to choose between having one's actions guided by feelings or by thoughts.[40] Those people who are at the lower end of the scale react mostly to feelings. They have less choice in their behaviors.

Michael Kerr describes the scale in this way. The scale is set at 0 to 100. In the range 0–25, a person lives in a feeling world. That person has a good deal of anxiety and most of her or his energy goes into loving or being loved. In the range of 25–50, people have a poor concept of self but are beginning to be able to differentiate. They look to outside authorities and are sensitive to other's feelings. They seek approval and are very susceptible to the spread of anxiety. In the 50–75 range, some decisions are thought-based and people have an awareness of the differences between thoughts and feelings. People in this range have more choice. Group anxiety produces symptoms in this group, but recovery is quicker. In the

75–100 range, a person is principle-oriented and goal-directed. This person lives in a world of choices and can adapt to chronic anxiety and stress. There are not many people in this range, and Bowen described the upper levels of this range as theoretical.[41]

There are two ways that an understanding of differentiation can be helpful in congregational ministry. The first is that the concept of differentiation provides a way to understand the behavior of both lay and clergy in a manner that is not pejorative. Daniel Papero writes, "The concept of differentiation eliminates the need for a concept of normalcy. Any level on the continuum is both natural and normal."[42] There is a tendency in congregational work to make value judgments on the behavior of both lay and clergy. Behavior is interpreted as a threat that perhaps is not a threat but rather the way an individual functions within a relationship.

Clergy often say things like, "Mrs. Doe always attacks clergy; she is always critical." Explanations are given, such as, "You know, she has deep personal problems," or she is described as a "leaping, psychotic clergy killer." As was said earlier, motivation is not a profitable area for exploration. She may or may not have deep personal problems or be a "clergy killer," but her reactivity is dictated by her level of differentiation and by the anxiety level of the system. Understood in this way, the behavior can be accounted for, acknowledged, and then responded to in a non-emotionally reactive way. Her behavior is not seen as automatically abnormal, but simply as the way in which she functions in this system and situation. Once you can anticipate an individual's reaction and it is no longer a surprise, then your response can be less reactive and more thought-based.

It is often discovered that Mrs. Doe always complains, and not just about the clergy, but about her family and work as well. On the other hand, if the problem is systemic in nature, and if, by some miracle, Mrs. Doe leaves the church, you will simply have another person take her place and her attitudes. None of this is to say that people at the lower end of the scale are mentally impaired, sick, dysfunctional or that they have more problems in life or on the job, or that they are not competent. The scale only gives indications that people at the lower end of the scale are more prone to reactivity, anxiety, and stress. They have more problems dealing with crisis, and they require more time to recover.

The second way a scale of differentiation becomes helpful is in understanding the relatedness of clergy and congregation. Often you hear congregations and clergy talk about each other as if they were different species. "They" did this or "she" did that are some of the phrases heard in and about congregations. The truth is that there is no "they" or "she" there is only *we*. People tend to marry and have relationships in the range of their functioning.[43] Friedman goes on to say that this range of functioning is far more important than culture or other compatibilities. What this means for understanding the congregation and its leadership is that, if the leadership of a congregation is emotional, unthinking, reactive, and handles crisis poorly, then the congregation will likely be the same, and the reverse is true. Ministers and congregations are attracted to each other based on their range of functioning, assuming they have any choice in the calling process.

In his book on ministry, Edward Schillebeeckx speaks of this close relationship between congregation and leader in another context. A minister's call is validated by having a congregation call that minister.[44] The congregation is validated by having a minister accept its call.[45] Schillebeeckx goes on to say that within the early church there was no "essential distinction between laity and ministers." This is the same point, in another discipline, that Bowen and others are making in terms of differentiation. Between laity and ministers in a given congregation, there is no essential difference in their range of functioning. If either the minister or the congregation was at a different point on the scale of differentiation they would not be attracted to each other. In the calling and coming, each validates the other's ministry.

Triangles

As originally understood, a triangle is the way that three people or groups of people relate to each other on emotional issues. This is considered one of the basic building blocks of human relationship. The original triangle is found in the family among mother, father, and child. Bowen felt that it was so basic that it probably also operated in animal societies.[46] The concept of triangles was later expanded to include the possibility of including an issue as one of the legs of the triangle.[47] In a congregational situation, an example of this might be minister + governing body + building committee or minister + head of women's group + lay person. The combinations are almost endless.

Triangles are a result of the emotional tension between two people. A third person is brought in to adjust the level of tension. During periods of calm, two of the people in the triangle are close and the third is on the outside. The twosome works to maintain this togetherness. In times of stress, triangles become more visible. In times of calm, the preferred position is as one of the twosome, but in times of stress it is in the outside position of the triangle. If the three members of the triangle are unable to handle the stress of the relationship and the emotional issues involved, then a fourth person will be brought in to form two interlocking triangles and to attempt to handle the emotional issues in this manner.[48]

Triangles are in a constant state of flux. In times of calm the outside person tries to get closer and in times of stress everyone tries to be the outside person or bring in someone else. This movement is all automatic and without thought. This process continues until families and organizations become a series of interlocking triangles. As tension shifts from triangle to triangle, it will eventually come

Triangles

A.

Triangles Happen
B. Triangles are learned
C. Triangles are generated by anxiety
D. Triangles involve being caught in the middle

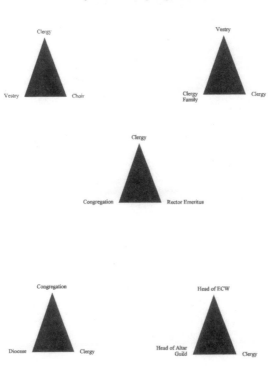

to rest in one triangle that becomes highly agitated, while the others return to calm.[49]

In triangles, there are two important variables. The first is differentiation and the second is the level of anxiety present in the system.[50] The lower the level of differentiation, the more intense the triangle; and the higher the level of anxiety, the more automatic and intense is the triangle.

The concept of triangles has several implications for congregational ministry. Friedman says that the concept of triangles goes a long way in explaining why things don't change when a single person enters or leaves the system. The system of interlocking triangles keeps the emotional issues constant and militates against change. Change can only be effected when the relationships and behaviors within the system are changed. This becomes a much larger project than changing one church member. One of the universal rules of triangles is that the more you try to change the behavior of others, the more it remains the same; also the stress level will rise in the person trying to make changes in others, for that person is taking on the stress of the relationship.[51]

How, then, can the system be changed? One way is through information. If a person can see the role they play in a system of triangles, often they can make a thoughtful choice in that role and lessen their stress by refusing to take the stress of others. (**Ministry Tip:** Don't step in front of the bullet if it doesn't have your name on it.) Stress becomes positional and a person can choose to change their position and thus his or her stress level. In understanding his or her role in a system of triangles, a person can understand the role of others, and less blaming takes place. If one person in a triangle can control his or her stress and automatic reactions and still remain in touch with the other two, then the overall reactivity will lessen. Working with a highly reactive congregation becomes a process of lessening the automatic functioning and increasing the intellectual control a person has over his or her own actions. The whole congregation becomes less reactive as more and more people become able to see the functioning of triangles and the roles they play in the system and choose to make stress-reducing choices.

Generational Transmission

One of the central concepts of natural systems theory, and one which sets it apart from other family theories, is the understanding that we will always have the past with us. This is not just a remembrance, but it is an *anamnesis*. The past participates in our present. Emotional responses, both in their nature and in their intensity, are passed down from previous generations.[52] Each family or group has a basic level of anxiety and way of coping with that anxiety that are passed on to each succeeding generation. Members of each generation are not independent actors starting afresh; a family is a multi-generational continuum. Peter Steinke describes this process as a relay race in which the torch of emotional process is passed from generation to generation.[53] The torch that you get is the torch that your family passes on, which may not be the torch you would choose or the torch you want.

This understanding of multi-generational process is also true of organizations and institutions. Friedman talks in terms of plum and pill congregations. Some congregations have three leaders in one hundred years; others have three leaders in three years. Changing either the clergy or individual members appears not to change the overall character of the congregation. Plums stay plums, and pills stay pills.[54] Multi-generational process provides a new way of looking at the functioning of congregations. Looking into how a congregation was started and the family processes of those founding members becomes a highly profitable exercise. Did they begin out of conflict? Was there a lot of emotional turmoil? Answers to these and similar questions can provide insight into the current conditions and processes, actions and reactions of a congregation.

This way of understanding how a congregation functions provides an alternative to the single-person or single-event cause of congregational problems. Utilizing natural systems theory to work with these congregations suggests that solutions are to be found in differentiation of leadership and in finding new ways to handle congregational anxiety. This often involves education and reflection, which help to change automatic processes into more thought-based processes.

Projection Process

This is the understanding that the problems of one person are often projected onto another. In families, the problems of the parents are sometimes projected onto the children. One parent may be over involved with one of the children. This can be a way of displacing anxiety between the parents and moving that anxiety to another generation.[55] This process can take place among many generations, moving anxiety from one generation to another until you have not only your own anxiety to deal with, but several generations of anxiety as well. This process also operates in congregations as congregational problems are projected onto one member, staff, or group as a way of dealing with anxiety. The problem is that by focusing on others, where nothing can be done, the opportunity to focus on self, where something can be done, is lost, and the problems are never solved.

Functional Position

What a person says, thinks, feels, and does is to some extent determined by the position that he or she occupies within the system and within a triangle.[56] The person may amplify, dampen, or generate anxiety. The person may be seen as problem creators or problem solvers. One of the benefits of this understanding of a person's role in a congregation is that it is not blameworthy, it just is. In addition, if you remove a problem person, someone else in the system will just assume that function, so there is no net gain. This understanding encourages people to focus on the process and not on individuals.

Emotional Cutoff

Emotional cutoff is a way in which people manage the intensity of the emotional process within a generation. The greater the fusion or undifferentiation between generations, the more likely a cutoff will occur: parents cut off from children and children from parents.[57] This same process occurs in congregations that are highly undifferentiated or fused. Members feel that they must either have their way or they must leave, "cut off" the congregation. People leave congregations seeking to be different. But when pressure mounts in their new congregation, the old behavior patterns will assert themselves. Cutoffs provide some immediate relief, but no long term solutions.

A more effective solution involves more objectivity.[58] If persons can gain emotional objectivity regarding the parts they play in a system and the ways they affect the overall functioning of the system, then real change and health is possible. Persons are able to stay in contact with the system and to change their behavior. This, in turn, can affect the functioning of the entire system, decreasing anxiety and emotional distance.

Conclusions

A natural systems understanding of congregations has some implications for the congregational leadership. Nonlinear thinking encourages an understanding of leadership that is relational. Leaders and members mutually affect each other. The actual position of leader is one of function rather than one based in natural precedence or a hierarchy of order. The function of leaders is most basically to take responsibility for their own actions, as the function of members is to take responsibility for their actions.

Friedman identifies some qualities that can be found in leaders who utilize natural systems thinking.[59] Leaders stay in touch with all members of their congregations, not just those whom they like and agree with, or those who support them. Leaders strive to be nonreactive in their stance. The leaders' positions are thought-based, as are their reactions to the positions of others. Disagreements are tolerated and are focused on positions taken, not on the persons who take these positions.

Finally, according to Friedman, the leader needs to be prepared to handle sabotage in a nonreactive manner while staying in touch with the saboteur. A leader's reactivity only increases the reactivity in the congregation. Emotionally cutting off from the congregation increases triangles and turns a democratic leader into a hierarchical head.[60] Friedman said that if there was one thing that he had not stressed enough, it was the loneliness and difficulty inherent in pursuing the path of leadership utilizing a natural systems theory approach.[61] Utilizing a natural systems approach may be effective, but it is time consuming, difficult, and lonely.

In this understanding of leadership, no one thing is more important than the health of the leader. In order to be non-reactive and in contact with all segments of the congregation, while not being engulfed, ministers need to place their health at the top of their priorities. Surfing may be a better choice than going to a guild meeting. An extra day off may be a better choice than having a well-crafted sermon. Remember, in a process or systems understanding of congregational ministry, no one event, meeting, or service is so important that it can't be missed—even Reformation Sunday. The primary job of the leader is to stay healthy. If this happens, then the congregation will stay healthy.

Ultimately, natural systems theory is about having choices and taking responsibility for those choices. It is about choosing to react out of a thought-based mode rather than the mode of primal urges. It is about choosing to be freed from generational patterns. It is about building self and then taking responsibility for self. It is about choosing to be the person we want to be and can be. It is about choosing to be the congregation we want and can be. It is about letting go the things we cannot change in ourselves and others.

This is not an easy path to take as we come to grapple with our own family issues and processes and the issues and processes of our congregations. The greatest obstacle in the way of this type of leadership is anxiety: the anxiety that is always present in ourselves

and the anxiety that is present in the congregation. The
congregation is, in fact, an anxiety-producing machine.

Chapter 4 – De Oratione

What is prayer? A visitor to one Episcopal church, was so carried away with the need to pray that he stood up and shouted, "praise the Lord!" Immediately, two ushers ran up the aisle to the person and said, "Please, we don't do that here." Two of the most popular tracts available in many of the Episcopal churches are "About Being An Episcopalian" and "The Episcopal Church: Essential Facts." In neither of these booklets is prayer, as a category or section, mentioned. The only mention of prayer in these booklets is in the section about the liturgy or as part of a discussion of *The Book of Common Prayer*. For example, "Common Prayer is the prayer and worship used 'in common,' when the members of the fellowship are gathered together," or "*The Book of Common Prayer* is one of the finest collections of great prayers ever offered by human beings to God. Prayer is not a major topic in these booklets. In it are prayers suited to every need and occasion."[1]

What is prayer? *The Book of Common Prayer* of the Episcopal Church, in the Outline of the Faith or Catechism, states that there are prayers both with and without words. Of those prayers with words there are seven kinds. They are adoration, praise, thanksgiving, penitence, oblation, intercession, and petition.[2] No other mention is made of prayer without words. What is prayer? In much of the public teachings of the Episcopal Church, it is something that is done: devotions to be undertaken; prayers for every occasion. It is not discussed as a practice or a discipline.

That there is more to prayer is hinted at obliquely in the teachings and publications of the church as in the possibility of prayers without words. Also the idea that God draws forth from us a response and this response is called prayer can be found in the catechism. More than a mention of this possibility is not to be found. Spirituality is left to the individual in the privacy of one's own home. This understanding of prayer and spirituality is not unique to the Episcopal Church. Many of the commonly called mainline denominations emphasize corporate worship, public oral prayer, and acts of charity as the core of their religious traditions.

This has not always been the case. There has been a long tradition within the Christian Church of prayer without words, of prayer that is more than a list of requests or thanksgivings. That is prayer of *being* not of *doing*, prayer of relationship. This tradition of silent prayer was, for a long time, forgotten, ignored, or relegated to the monasteries of the Roman Catholic tradition.

Prior to the fifteenth century, a positive attitude existed toward methods of contemplative prayer within the Christian Church. These methods of contemplation had been brought to the West from the desert fathers and mothers by John Cassian and had become a part of Western spirituality, incorporated into the teachings of the monastic orders.[3] After the sixteenth century, there was an increasingly negative attitude toward the methods of contemplation. There were several reasons for this change in attitude by the church.

First, what had been considered a single prayer, the practice of *Lectio Divina*, consisted of meditation, *meditatio*, (reflection on the words of scripture), affective prayer, *oratio*, (spontaneous movement of the will), and contemplation, *contemplatio*, (resting in God); this was divided into three separate prayers.[4] Each of these prayers had its own aims and goals and developed its own followers and methods. The last, meditation, was seen as being reserved for saints and those who were truly close to God. As a result, the practice of meditation declined, even among the religious congregations. There was a general decline in popular spirituality during this period. The Reformation took place in this period, and the Protestant churches were formed without a general knowledge of meditative prayer. With the rejection by the Roman Catholic Church of the practices of affective prayer, that is *oratio*,[5] *Lectio Divina* as a popular practice was lost.

Second, within the Catholic tradition, great schools of prayer and practice were developed, including those of Ignatius, de Sales, and others. All of them were discursive techniques. Contemplation was pushed further into the background.[6] More and more, mysticism was seen as something for the few, not to be aspired to by the many. Mystical theology was seen as a discipline of interest only to a few scholars. But this had not always been the case.

Tradition

Mystical theology within the Christian tradition began with Clement of Alexandria.[7] Clement makes the connection between *gnosis* and mysticism and begins the process of mapping out the definitions and goals of the mystical journey. "The *Logos* of God was made man," says Clement, "so that you might learn how man can become God." One of the key terms that Clement defines and brings into Christianity is that of *apatheia*, or the calming of the passions.[8] On the more practical side, Clement combines the knowledge of *apatheia* with the practice of *apatheia*, so learning and praxis become a whole. Clement also divided biblical interpretation into two kinds, literal and spiritual. All of these definitions and understandings would later come together in the desert fathers and then find their way into the Western spiritual tradition.

The shaping of this tradition continues with Origen and his writings. Origen puts forth the idea that Jesus is in union with God, and that Jesus's followers can also enter into "friendship with God."[9] This is accomplished through a process of prayer involving several stages: *deesis*, asking for goods that are spiritual; *proseuke*, abandonment to pure relationship with God; and *doxologia*, in which we are absorbed into union with God.[10] The prayer of silence is introduced into Christian practice.

One of the most popular stories of the age of Christian practice was that of Antony, as told in a book by Athanasius. This story gripped the imagination of the ancient world. Antony's life became so famous and familiar that, by 400, only a few decades after its publication, it was already seen as a classic and Antony as a hero from the past.[11] It presents the life of Antony as one of conversion, struggle, dependence on Christ, and finally doing the work of Christ and, in some sense, becoming Christ.

This pattern is similar to the three stages in the journey of Origen. Dependence on Christ is similar to *deesis* in receiving spiritual gifts from God, *proseuke* is doing the work of Christ, and *doxologia* is becoming one with Christ in aim and deed, as in the Antony story. Antony reaches this end or union through what Clement called *apatheia*. In describing Antony after his purification through struggle, Athanasius writes, "The state of his soul was one of purity, for it was not constricted by grief, nor relaxed by pleasure, nor affected by either laughter or dejection."[12] Antony was not alone in this experience and practice. At one time there were over 50,000 people in the desert having similar experiences. Antony's hermitage had become a city.

The person who brought this method of this desert practice and experience to the West was John Cassian. Owen Chadwick writes that Cassian "was the first guide to the contemplative ideal in the history of Western thought."[13] Cassian envisioned a ladder of contemplation ending on the highest rung, that of the contemplation of the one alone.[14] Cassian's chief contribution to history was to bring these understandings and practices from the desert East to the urban West. Philip Rousseau writes that much of what Cassian did was to modify and interpret Eastern ascetic traditions for Western readers.[15] By writing in Latin, Cassian was able to separate Greek philosophical terms from their Gnostic, Platonist, or Stoic roots and thus make them more palatable to the orthodox church. Cassian's writings became part of the Western monastic tradition.

Thomas Keating says that this tradition was summed up at the end of the sixth century by Gregory the Great. Gregory described contemplation as, "Knowledge of God that is impregnated with love." Keating says that Gregory understood this prayer as both a result of reflecting on scripture and a gift from God. Gregory called this final state of prayer "resting in God."[16]

Lectio Divina

Over the centuries, the monks developed a tradition of prayer that consisted of *Lectio Divina*, which means divine reading.[17] This is a practice that includes both reading and listening to scripture. Its most salient characteristic is the immense reverence for the word of God.[18] This practice of prayer consists of three parts, *meditatio*, *oratio*, and *contemplatio*.

The first of these, *meditatio*, is a reasoning process where the words of scripture are carefully considered and reflected upon in order to seek out some personal meaning.[19] This first step is a function of the intellect. The second, *oratio*, is harder to define. It is an active effort to keep one's heart open to God in prayer. Thomas Keating calls this stage of prayer a spontaneous movement of the will in response to the reflections on scripture in *meditatio*. This may include assent to and practice of the moral values discovered in reflection. Finally, *contemplatio* is what Gregory the

Great called "resting in God." These three stages of prayer can all take place in one time period of prayer.

In the sixteenth century, this one prayer became divided into three types of prayers: discursive, if the thinking process was emphasized; affective, if acts of the will were emphasized; and mystical, if infused grace was the chief characteristic.[20] Each of these types of prayer had its own set of rules, methods, and goals. This had the practical effect of relegating contemplation or infused grace to the realm of the monastic or the spiritual professionals. *Contemplatio* was not something to which the average Christian could aspire. This was the understanding at the time of the Reformation. With the suppression of the monasteries, the tradition was almost lost.[21] However, the tradition was kept alive, in practice, among those in the monasteries, and knowledge of it was kept alive among those in seminaries and universities.

Revival
In the early 1970s, there was a wave of revival and renewal sweeping through churches in the United States. Many of the denominations were examining their liturgies in light of new studies of the early church. The Roman Catholic denomination was undergoing a transformation caused by Vatican II. There was a new openness sweeping the churches. A small group of Trappist monks from St. Joseph's Abbey in Spencer, Massachusetts, were thinking about what contribution they might make to this renewal. They had thought that, with Vatican II, they would see a return of young people to the Church. Instead, many of the young people looked toward the East for spiritual wisdom, seeking help from a variety of gurus, swamis, and roshi. They often traveled long distances to India, Thailand, or Sri Lanka in search of knowledge and practice. Others imported spiritual masters or found answers from the sharing of returning disciples.[22]

The question that arose in the mind of Keating was why those young people weren't coming to see them. The answer was that they didn't know there was a Christian form of contemplation. Thomas Keating, Basil Pennington, William Meninger, and others began to investigate these practices and teachers with which the young people were involved. They went out and attended meetings of these groups, talked with the teachers, and then invited them back to the monastery.[23] Keating challenged his chapter to find a way to adapt the teachings of the Christian tradition for the modern world. Keating realized that what was good for a monk might not be applicable to an active life.[24]

William Meninger began to investigate ancient methods of Christian prayer. It was felt that *Lectio Divina* took too much time and required the monastery environment; a simpler and shorter form was needed. Meninger developed a form of prayer and began to teach it to the priests in the monastery. Pennington began to give workshops in the method at Spencer's guest house to both clergy and lay. Keating moved to St. Benedict's in Snowmass, Colorado, and began to distill Meninger's work into the method for centering prayer. Later, with Gustave Reininger, he began to develop an organization to teach centering prayer in the parishes.

Prayer: The Way to Relationship
One of the essential understandings of centering prayer is that it is possible to have a relationship with God. This relationship, like any other, grows and flowers in direct proportion to the effort that is put into it and the time that is devoted to it. It is possible for prayer to be more than a petition or thanksgiving. Prayer is the avenue toward friendship or fellowship with God.

This idea of relationship is not new, but, in fact, is the very core belief of Christianity. Its roots are in the Bible and in the sacrament of baptism. "Where does centering prayer come from?" asks Keating. His reply is, from the indwelling holy Trinity that comes with the grace of baptism.[25] St. Paul writes in Galatians 2:20, "It is no longer I that live, but Christ who lives in me." Pennington comments on this passage saying that we have been not only created by God, but re-created in Christ, and Christ in us. We have been baptized into the love of Christ.[26]

This tradition comes from the Eastern church through its major writers such as Clement, Origen, Evagrius, the Cappadocian fathers, Athanasius, and John Cassian. It is continued in the Western European tradition in the works of Bernard of Clairvaux and William de Thierry, Pseudo-Dionysius, Meister Eckhart, the author of *The Cloud of Unknowing*, Theresa of Avila, and John of the Cross.

All of these works are encompassed in the twentieth-century writings of Pennington, Keating, and Meninger. Pennington writes that the only new things about centering prayer are the name and the packaging.[27] This is still an important contribution because it provides a way for the teachings and experiences of the early Eastern Christians to be accessible to the modern world. It provides a pre-mechanistic worldview of religion that fits well in a post-mechanistic world. Science finally catches up with religion. It provides an alternative to a cause-and-effect religion. Instead of a person's relationship with God being based on doing or not doing particular actions, or saying particular prayers or performing particular acts of worship, the relationship itself is what is important and what is nurtured through time spent with God in prayer. It is time spent getting to know God. Basil Pennington describes this experience of being with God. "In our relationship with God, too, beyond all doing and talking and thinking there need to be times when we are simply present to him in the fullness of our being, experiencing the immediacy of his loving and life-giving presence to us."[28]

The Process of Relationship

Thomas Keating sees a parallel between the way we form human relationships and the way we can form a relationship with God.[29] In the beginning, when we first meet someone, we want to know more about them, so we seek to find out what they like and what they don't like, how they spend their time and things like that. Our relations with them are formal, perhaps, in restricted social settings.

Our relationship with God is begun in the same manner. We seek to find out about God through reading the scriptures, which tell a person about God's acts in history and about God's likes and dislikes. This is like the beginning of *Lectio Divina*. A person's relationship with God at this point is formal, often expressed in verbal communication in prayers that have been written by others or in formal worship services. Prayers are repeated by rote. Keating calls this stage "acquaintanceship."

This may lead to the next stage, which is "friendliness." In human relationships, people spend more time together and in more informal settings sharing a bit with each other. In *Lectio Divina*, a person begins to reflect on the scriptures and the values that are contained within. He or she begins to learn the Christian life.

The next stage is that of "friendship." Here, in human relationships, a person decides to make a commitment. "I am going to spend time with this person." They may have to rearrange their lives to make space for the other person, but they choose to do this. In *Lectio Divina*, a person responds to the reading of the scriptures with spontaneous prayer, acts of love, adoration, or petition. It is at this point that people begin to practice the Christian life and to make the moral values of scripture their own. It is here that people want to make a commitment to Christ and to the Christian way of life.

In the last stage in human relationships, people just want to spend time in each other's presence. Nothing needs to happen. No event needs to be planned. Just being there is enough. In *Lectio Divina*, the word of God is assimilated in silence. In the Christian life a person's actions are directed by Christ's will. There is union between God and humankind. This is the *theoria* of Clement and the *henosis* of Origen. It is not restricted to a few saints in monasteries, but is available to all called by God, baptized in Christ, and empowered by the Holy Spirit.

Roadblocks

Standing in the way of union with God is a person's understanding of self. Basil Pennington expresses it this way: "We experience our contingency and desperately want to create or find something on which we can depend. Unfortunately we look in the wrong direction."[30] The place that we look is outside ourselves to the material world. We construct a false self based on our needs for security, control, power, affection, and esteem.[31]

Thomas Keating explains the reason for this false self system as human beings coming to consciousness without union with God.[32] The result of this is alienation from God and from each other. Human beings, then, create for themselves an identity from the material goods at hand, hoping to find the security that is found only in God. In practical terms, this is played out in childhood as disappointments and frustrations lead to the creation of a false self that seeks happiness in satisfying the instinctual needs of security control, power, affection, and esteem.[33] Human beings carry these programs for happiness into adulthood, often with disastrous results. People want to control every situation, win every contest and be universally loved. But, with a world filled with billions of other people striving for the same goals, the odds for success become minuscule. Programs for happiness become programs for failure. Most people are not aware that these programs are forming and shaping their decisions and actions.

This is the reason that intellectually choosing to follow the values of the Gospel often meets with frustration and failure. People may make conscious choices, but they are thwarted by their unconscious desires. Patterns that were formed in childhood continue unconsciously in adulthood. "The heart of the Christian *ascesis* is the struggle with our unconscious motivations," says Keating.[34] Changing lifestyles won't help because you bring your false self with you.

Symptoms
One of the signs of these unconscious programs is the emotions that accompany their frustration. Evagrius Ponticus was the first to note these and to categorize them. Evagrius listed them as gluttony, impurity, avarice, sadness, anger, restlessness, vainglory, and pride.[35] It is these emotions that are most felt in congregational ministry. These emotions buffet and consume both lay and clergy alike.

Gluttony causes people to seek after material goods as signs of self-worth and to find reasons why sacrifice is not necessary in the life of the church. Impurity causes people to lust after bodies, seeking to gain an increased value in self in the satisfying of sexual desires. This also leads a person to seek power through sexual conquests. It can also be just the overwhelming desire for anything. Avarice is chronic anxiety brought into the present. The desire to possess things now as a hedge against a future that may never come. Sadness is the longing for things not possessed: I would be happy if only....Anger is the reaction when our aims are thwarted, whether for the acquisition of something or control of someone. Restlessness is a dissatisfaction with the way things are; the desire to move from place to place and thing to thing without ever finding satisfaction in anything. Vainglory causes people to seek the praise of others over all else: the approval of the group is everything. Pride causes people to place their trust in themselves and to deny the role of God in their lives. To change this situation in life requires more than assent to new values; it requires an interior change that begins with repentance, which is another way of saying to look for happiness in a new place.

The Divine Therapy

A preacher once described the Eucharist as the medicine of immortality bestowing God's gift of everlasting life. Keating describes centering prayer as the divine therapy bestowing God's gift of grace for healing in this life.[36] The illness that all of humankind suffers from is that of original sin. In classical terms, original sin is defined, as represented by Tertullian, "And the man being given over to death on account of his sin, the entire human race, tainted in their descent from him, were made a channel for transmitting his condemnation."[37] A more modern understanding can be represented by Keating who describes original sin as "A way of explaining the universal experience of coming to full reflective self-consciousness without the inner conviction or experience of union with God."[38] The effects of this sin, Keating goes on to say, are three: illusion, which is the inability to seek happiness in ways that humans were created to find happiness; concupiscence, which is looking for happiness in the wrong places; and weakness of will, which is the inability to pursue happiness where it may be found.[39] The divine therapy seeks to address these effects of original sin.

The Process of Healing

The process by which the therapy works is called *Ad lumen per crucem*. What is crucified is the false self through the process of purgation. This is not a new theory, but one which has a long history within the Christian church. This is the way of the desert fathers and mothers, of Evagrius Ponticus, John Cassian, Bonaventure, Theresa of Avila, and John of the Cross; it is a way that continues down to the present day in the method of centering prayer.

Keating writes of four distinct moments that are found in the divine therapy. The first moment takes place when a person sits down and begins to pray. It is an assent to the will of God. It is a willingness to be converted. Clebsch describes this willingness as convertibility in his preface to the *Life of Antony* and calls it the first step on Antony's journey towards sanctification.

The second moment is produced by the first. It is a state of rest, a sense of God's presence, a peace or interior silence. Keating calls this "deep rest."[40] There is a feeling of the presence of God. It is at this point that God becomes the therapist in the sense that a person places trust in God and looks to God for that love and trust that was not received in childhood, a sort of divine transference. The third moment is that of unloading, where the defense mechanisms relax and the thoughts and emotions of the unconscious come to the surface.

The fourth moment is that of evacuation, where the emotional pain is moved out and space is opened up within the person. More of the divine presence is revealed within, and the person is closer to his or her center. Gustave Reininger sees this process as similar to that of Bonaventure's purgation, illumination, and perfective union.[41]

The practical result of this prayer is that unconscious patterns of behavior that had been present from childhood and the emotions that accompanied these patterns are gradually replaced with more constructive behavior. This happens when a person comes to realize their true self as a child of God who is divinely loved and whose self-worth does not rest on overwhelming desires for security, control, power, affection, and esteem. The hurts of childhood can be put behind, and a new life in union with Christ can begin.

The Method

The guidelines for centering prayer were developed by Thomas Keating as a way to bring centuries of Christian traditions of prayer into the modern era.[42] Centering prayer should be practiced twice a day, once in the morning and once in the evening. following the guidelines. There are four guidelines or steps for centering prayer:

> 1. Choose a sacred word as the symbol of your intention to consent to God's presence and action within.

> 2. Sitting comfortably and with eyes closed, settle briefly and silently introduce the sacred word as the symbol of your consent to God's presence and action within.

> 3. When you become aware of thoughts, return ever-so-gently to the sacred word.

> 4. At the end of the prayer period, remain in silence with eyes closed for a couple of minutes.[43]

The first guideline is to choose a sacred word. This word is symbolic of a person's desire to be in the presence of God and to surrender to God's action in their lives. This word is not sacred in itself, but rather it is sacred because it is symbolic of a person's intent to be with God. It is best to choose a word of one syllable so the word itself does not become a distraction. Words such as abba, love, holy, Jesu, peace, and amen are examples of sacred words that people have chosen. Having chosen a word it is best to stay with that word for several prayer sessions.

The second guideline is to sit comfortably and introduce the sacred word as a symbol of consent to God. One should choose a comfortable position which may be sitting on a chair or on the floor using a cushion or prayer bench. The eyes are closed, and the things that are happening in the world around the person, as well as the things that are inside of the person praying, are gently released and recede in importance and emotional attachment. This is a passive form of prayer, and the word is introduced very gently. Keating describes this process of introduction as laying a feather on a piece of absorbent cotton. Sometimes during the course of prayer the word becomes vague or even disappears altogether so that in the end only the intention to be with God remains.

The third guideline is to return to the sacred word when the person praying becomes aware of thoughts. Thoughts in this case mean perceptions, feelings, images, memories, reflections, outside noises, or interior commentaries. Thoughts are inevitable and normal, but as long as no emotional energy is attached to them the thoughts will disappear.

Keating compares this process to a river filled with boats. The river of consciousness is filled with the boats of everyday life. These boats are made of feelings, experiences, and emotions. The surface of this river is like our daily life. In order for the sunlight to penetrate beneath the surface, the boats need to be cleared from the river. The sacred word is like a log that is floated down the river to clear the boats from the surface. Soon only the log remains, then it floats away. The river is clear and light can penetrate into the depth of the river and reach our true self.[44] The practice for this guideline can be summed up in the four R's:

1. **Resist** no thought.　　2. **Retain** no thought.

3. **React** emotionally to no thought.　　4. **Return** ever-so-gently to the sacred word.

The fourth guideline is to remain in silence for several minutes at the completion of the prayer. This allows a time for the attention to gradually return and focus on the world around it. It is a period of transition that allows the person praying to bring the silence of the prayer into their daily lives.

Teaching Centering Prayer in the Congregation
Introducing centering prayer to a congregation involves teaching both method and practice. The easier of the two is method, which takes only a few minutes to learn, following the guidelines. The more difficult of the two is establishing a practice for those just learning the prayer. Prayer does not work unless you practice. Instruction in centering prayer is designed to encourage and support practice.

The Beginning
In starting a centering prayer ministry it is best to begin by meeting with the church leadership, both lay and ordained, so they have some understanding of the tradition, the method, and what happens during the prayer period. Sitting in a room for long periods of time in a group with your eyes closed, even without incense and candles, might be considered strange by some. Time spent in education about centering prayer at the beginning is time well spent. In addition, there needs to be one person who is responsible for the organization of the group in the congregation and can also act as group leader. A second person is needed to assist the group leader so the demands on the time of the leader do not become overwhelming. A third person to do hospitality is helpful; they can unlock doors, set the room, and provide whatever refreshments are necessary. This allows the leader to concentrate on teaching and leading the group.

Starting the group itself is a three-step process involving an introductory workshop, follow-up meetings, and teaching *Lectio*

Divina. The time period for this process is seven weeks. After this time period, those who wish to continue the practice with a group can break up into small ongoing groups consisting of seven to twelve people. The three people leading the initial session—the leader, assistant leader and hospitality person—can each lead one of the ongoing groups if there are that many people who want to continue.

The Introductory Workshop

The introductory workshop is the first public step in starting a centering prayer group in a congregation. The workshop should be led by someone who practices centering prayer and who is a trained presenter in the method. The workshop can be presented as a single six-hour session, a two-day weekend program, or any four-session period.

The workshop includes four sessions of forty-five minutes each and two twenty-minute sessions of centering prayer. The first workshop covers prayer as the process of having a relationship with God and the history of the contemplative tradition within the Christian church.

The second workshop consists of teaching the method of centering prayer. First, the guidelines are reviewed, and then twenty minutes of practice takes place. After the practice, the people in the workshop are encouraged to share their experiences, and any questions that arise are answered. Some questions that have been asked include: What happens if I go to sleep? Why can't I stop thinking thoughts? Why did nothing happen for me? The leaders address these question as best they can.

The third workshop is about the role of thoughts, emotions, and distractions in centering prayer. In this session, time is spent reassuring people that their thoughts are normal and that the practice of centering prayer is a process, not something achieved in one session. Instead, each session of prayer is unique and valuable in itself. Some sessions of prayer have more thoughts than others. In addition to thoughts, feelings and emotions are discussed, and ways of letting go of these feelings and emotions during the time of prayer are topics that are covered. This letting go is called the unloading of the unconscious or the process of interior purification.

The fourth workshop covers the fruits of centering prayer and methods for bringing the benefits of prayer into daily life. There is no direct or linear connection between prayer and the benefits of prayer. The effects of centering prayer are found in the whole of the way a person lives their life. The fruits of centering prayer may include more silence in a person's life and less reactivity. Other fruits may include improvement in relationships and a desire to reach out to others. Methods for extending centering prayer into daily life are methods for intentionally living a life in Christ; these include such simple, practical things as making *Lectio Divina* part of daily life, choosing a short sentence to repeat while walking or doing chores, or maybe carrying a book of scriptural passages that remind a person of their commitment to God. These methods can also include cultivating a basic acceptance of oneself, practicing unconditional acceptance of others, and letting go of excessive group identification.

The Weekly Sessions

The weekly sessions of centering prayer are built around a twenty-minute practice of the prayer itself. This is the second step of the teaching process. The sessions should last an hour and a half. Each session is opened with two or three minutes of reading scripture, followed by a twenty-minute practice of centering prayer. The practice itself is opened and closed by the ringing of a bell. At the end of the practice, the Lord's Prayer is said slowly by the leader.

Following the prayer practice, a video is shown or a book is read about centering prayer or the contemplative tradition. After this session, time is spent sharing experiences of the practice of prayer during the week and the effects in people's lives. Each session may be closed with refreshments and a time spent in fellowship.

Lectio Divina

The third step in the process is a session on *Lectio Divina*. The purpose of this session is to establish firmly the practice of centering prayer in the mainstream of Christian tradition. It is shown how centering prayer is a means of facilitating *contemplatio*. This is taught last, after the practice of centering prayer has been established, since it can be a separate practice in itself. The complete method of *Lectio* is taught at this time.

The Effects of Centering Prayer in the Congregation

Centering prayer can affect the functioning of the congregation in several ways. Centering prayer can lower the overall reactivity of the congregation through lowering the reactivity of the individual members. Prayer can also help to alleviate the effects of the physiological changes that are brought about by reactivity and anxiety. As people who practice the prayer begin to heal from their emotional hurts, there is less confusion over their own emotional issues and those that might be projected onto others. As a person's relationship with God deepens through prayer, they feel more secure in being open with others.

The practice of prayer can lead a person toward an unconditional acceptance of others as they learn to recognize their own drives for control, power, security, affection, and esteem. Prayer also helps to dismantle the over-identification with groups such as the choir, Christian education, and others. As a person comes to rely more on God, he or she is able to let go of the other groups and beliefs that he or she took on to bolster their concept of self. And finally, through their growing relationship with God, people begin to take on the values that are found in God's Word and the behavior that these values engender.

Chapter 5 – Centering Prayer and Systems Theory

I do not understand my own actions.
For I do not do what I want,
but I do the very thing I hate.

Rom. 7:15

Natural Systems Theory

When I returned from summer vacation, there was a call waiting for me from the minister of the church next to mine. I called him back. He told me that he had resigned from his church and he was going to retire from the ministry. Now, fifteen years later, I can't remember what the issue was. In general, the church governing board wanted him to ask their permission to do something he felt was his prerogative. In fact, this was not new, but a common occurrence with this board. He said that he had tried to call me and another minister. We had both been gone on vacation. So he resigned.

In talking with this minister, it seemed there was no particular reason he resigned from his church that evening. Nothing new had happened. He had just "had enough." Over the next several years, I noticed more and more similar cases in which the minister resigned because he had had enough. I also heard of several cases where the minister was fired because the congregation had had enough. Enough what? I wanted to know. Sometimes I asked. The reply was pretty much always the same: "Just enough," they said.

In some of these cases, there was not an apparent cause; in others there seemed to be many causes. Often, the clergy blamed the laity and the laity blamed the clergy. The diocese or church administrative body usually chose a side, and set about the task of replacing the clergy or silencing the laity. In many cases, this strategy was not successful. The problems in the congregations continued for years and, in some cases, for generations. There was one church I knew of that had gone from over 1500 members to fewer than fifty in twenty-three years. Other churches, I found, had had four pastors in five years. Churches developed reputations as being "clergy killers." Clergy developed reputations as being "problems."

By the time I joined a diocesan staff, I was convinced that an incident-based understanding of church conflict was not adequate and certainly not successful. The publication of Edwin Friedman's book, *Generation to Generation*, seemed to offer an alternative to a single event or single incident theory of church problems and conflict. Drawing on the works of Murray Bowen, whose theory emerged from the treatment of family groups with a schizophrenic member, and was later used in marriage and family therapy, Friedman proposed that congregations operate as a family system.

In examining family relationships, Bowen wrote,

> *The total fabric of society, as it pertains to human illness, dysfunction, and misbehavior, is organized around the concept of man as an autonomous individual who controls his own destiny. When the observing lens is opened to include the entire family field, there is increasing evidence that man is not as*

> *separate from his family, from those about him, and*
> *from his multi-generational past as he has fancied*
> *himself to be.*[1]

Friedman took this understanding of family process and applied it to churches and synagogues. Friedman writes, "Everything that has been said thus far about emotional process in personal families is equally applicable to emotional process in churches, synagogues, rectories (which function as nuclear systems), and hierarchies (which function as extended systems). These too are families."[2] Friedman goes on to say that not only are churches families, but their members have families. This intensifies and complicates the emotional process. There is family process laid over family process.

Family interactions naturally produce anxiety.[3] The family and its members develop ways to absorb and bind this anxiety. Adaptations are made within the family structure. This process is created as part of our evolutionary heritage and can also be viewed in other life forms. But the anxiety produced in the balancing of our relationships can also produce problems. Anxiety problems are seen in family systems in which there is a member of the family who is schizophrenic or a member who "causes trouble." In institutions, these same symptoms can be observed as problem individuals or problem events, with statements such as: "This clergy person is a real loser," or "This art show demeans our church and our God." Rather than deal with the individual symptoms or events or people, it may be better to deal with the underlying cause.

Daniel V. Papero, in writing about organizations and institutions, suggests that instead of focusing on individuals and their habits, a more profitable approach might be to focus on the functioning of the organization itself. In examining that functioning, one will find that a basic underlying variable in all organizations is anxiety.[4] Within the organization, anxiety affects not only individuals, but also the organization itself. Papero goes on to say that anxiety is more than just a psychological state; it actually describes the condition of the individual or organization.[5] In an individual or organization, anxiety has a marked effect on the ability to function. Intensified anxiety can produce heightened sensitivity to others, shifts in perception, changes in the way events are interpreted, and an increase in behavior that is automatic rather than thought-based.[6]

The concept of a church as an emotional system which produces anxiety in the natural course of its relationships helps explain events, symptoms, and behaviors that surface in individual religious organizations. This understanding helps to explain what at times appear to be inexplicable courses of action taken by leaders and members of these organizations. Identifying and understanding the problem is only the first step. Time and energy can be saved by no longer engaging in unsuccessful programs for change that focus on the individual. There are no quick fixes or parts to be replaced. Instead, the relationships within the system need to be addressed in such a way that anxiety and frustration can be constructively managed and adjusted.

Centering Prayer

Once upon a time there was a large and wealthy church in a sylvan setting. It looked peaceful, a place of worship and rest. The new minister lasted less than two weeks. It was believed that the minister received a six-figure settlement to leave and both sides considered it money well spent. Thirteen days passed between the joy of a new arrival in ministry to uncivil war, acrimony, and recriminations. This was not a unique situation particular to this church or denomination. It was the church in the latter part of the twentieth century.

The minister came to the new pastorate with high hopes. The congregation shared these hopes. The minister who had left had been at the church a long time, but in recent years had been waiting for his retirement. The new minister was coming to get things going again. There had been a long and careful search process looking for just the right person. When the new minister arrived, he found several areas of the church, including an auxiliary organization, that were not under his direct control. When he tried to consolidate the different groups under his leadership, he met with resistance, then hostility, then opposition. He refused to back down because to do so would have been defeat. Besides, all areas of the church should be under his control. He had the right to make changes. Many in the congregation felt things were fine the way they were, for no other reason than they had been like that for years. What right did the new minister have to make substantial changes so quickly? He was endangering the very fabric of the church. If he continued, there would be no church left. Who did he think he was anyway?

Meetings were held. Secret meetings were held. Both sides retained lawyers. Within two weeks the congregation was looking for a new pastor. How did things go so badly so quickly? How did the situation escalate so fast? Why was the end so violent? Emotions escalated quickly out of control. The issues themselves were lost in what became verbal violence and confrontation. The battle became one for power, control, and esteem.

Various mediators who came into this situation began their work with a prayer or a prayer service. Visible effects of these oral prayers were not immediately evident. Perhaps a different method of prayer would have been more effective. *The Book of Common Prayer* of the Episcopal Church teaches about the kinds of prayer in the section "Catechism."

Q. *"What is Prayer"*
A. *"Prayer is responding to God, by thought and by deeds, with or without words."*

Church structures and organizations are, by their nature, rife with anxiety. Systems theory provides us with a way of understanding the processes at work within the congregation. But understanding congregational process and the anxiety that this process produces is not always enough. Many times we know how to act, we just don't seem to be able to act the way we desire. A prayer without words, centering prayer, provides us with an additional and complimentary way of understanding what is happening in the church and also an effective way of working with the anxiety and emotions that are found within a congregation. Centering prayer has the added benefit of having been taught in the church for over a thousand years. This makes it more accessible to church workers and leaders than natural systems theory. The combination of centering prayer and natural systems theory, when used together as complements, provide an effective model of church leadership and an effective avenue for congregational change.

Church writers and theologians have understood from the early centuries of Christianity that anxiety blocks relationship, both with God and with human beings. Early writers such as Origen and Clement write about anxiety and emotions. Other early writers like Evagrius Ponticus and John Cassian offer practical solutions and courses of action. The solution that they offer to this situation of anxiety and emotion is *apatheia* or the calming of passions which is achieved through silent prayer. Modern writers such as Thomas Keating and Basil Pennington continue to write on this theme in modern language for current times.

In his book *Invitation to Love*, Keating describes how our relationships with others are often governed by emotional processes or programs that begin with our relations with our parents in infancy. Most people, says Keating, are unaware that these programs are functioning and influencing their behavior and judgments.[7] These programs set off emotional responses and reactions. Soon, before we are actually consciously aware of the situation, a difference of opinion has escalated into a full-scale emotional conflict. Sides are taken, lines are drawn in the sand, and there is no turning back or backing down. Relationships are strained and broken.

Centering prayer is a prayer that is concerned with relationship: a person's relationship with God. As this relationship is strengthened through centering prayer, so also are one's relations with other people. Keating calls this process "Divine Therapy."[8] While the primary relationship addressed through centering prayer is with God, a side effect appears to be a healing of relationships with others. Centering prayer and natural systems theory share several understandings and view the world in similar ways.

Relationship and Process

> *Jesus said, "The first commandment is this: Hear O Israel The Lord our God is the only Lord. Love the Lord your God with all your heart, with all your soul, with all your mind, and with all your strength. The second is this: Love your neighbor as yourself. There is no other commandment greater than these.*[9]

One of the understandings that centering prayer and natural systems theory share is the importance of relationships. No individual person exists alone on an emotional island. In Christianity, the importance of relationship is symbolized by the understanding of God as Trinity. Hans Küng writes that in considering the Trinity we must reflect on the relationship between God and Jesus with reference to the Spirit.

Again, Küng writes about Father, Son, and Holy Spirit as a unity of operation and revelation.[10] God is in relationship with God's self and, through creation, calls humankind to be in relationship with God. The fall and salvation can be seen in terms of human beings attempting to sever their relationships with God, and God calling them back into relationship with God. In our estrangement from God we, as humans, also end up estranged from our neighbor.

> *You made us...and we turned against you...*
> *and we turned against one another.*
> *Again and again you called us to return.*[11]

Centering prayer and natural systems theory both place primacy on relationship. Sara Butler writes that "the practice of centering prayer is a common call to relationship."[12] Relationship with God, like relationships with other people, begins with dialogue. With God, sometimes our dialogue is formal and corporate, such as that which is found in our liturgy; at other times, it is personal and private. *The Book of Common Prayer* lists seven kinds of prayer: adoration, praise, thanksgiving, penitence, oblation, intercession, and petition. In some ways these are like our topics of conversation with other people. As relationships deepen, a point comes when words are not necessary; just being in relationship with the other is enough. So, too, is a relationship with God, and centering prayer provides a way to be in relationship through opening ourselves up to God's communication with us. Thomas Keating writes,

> *In time we will grow from a reflective relationship with God to one of communion. The latter is a being-to-being, presence-to-presence relationship, which is the knowledge of God in pure faith.*[13]

Centering prayer is a way of being in relationship with God. The fruits of centering prayer are being in relationship with human beings. All of God's creation is relationship and exists in relationship.

Systems theory also sees the inter-connectedness of the world. Peter Steinke writes, "Systems thinking is basically a way of thinking about life as all of a piece. It is a way of thinking about how the whole is arranged, how its parts interact, and how the relationships between the parts produce something new."[14] Natural systems theory begins with the understanding that all life is inter-connected and that relationship patterns and behaviors are shared by all life forms. This theory of the inter-connectedness of life was proposed by the sociobiologists who saw shared behavioral traits between animal species.[15] Murray Bowen made two major breaks with the thinking of the psychiatric community. The first was that the emotional functioning of humans was not particular to humans, but part of behavior patterns found in all animal life. To separate animal and human behaviors in functioning was to create an artificial dichotomy and to engage in intellectual constructs whose validity rested only in the human mind. Bowen's second discovery was that any understanding of human behavior must take into account the relationship system. In short, "Bowen proposed that the family operated in ways that were consistent with its being a system and that the system's principles of operation were rooted in nature."[16] Bowen himself extended this understanding of humans to groupings outside the family system, including work and social organizations. In describing these relationships, natural systems theory uses terms such as triangles, self-differentiation, family emotional systems, projection process, and multiple generation transmission process, all as ways of viewing and understanding human relationships. No person or their functioning can be considered on their own, but only in the context of their relationships both past and present.

The second area of similarity between centering prayer and natural systems theory is in the understanding of process. Much of

Western thinking has been informed by the concept of history as shaped by single great individuals or single important events. The view is that a single person, taking a single action, has single-handedly effected change. This mechanistic model was taken from the physical world. If one exerts force on an object, it moves until the energy transmitted dissipates. People are different from physical objects in that they interact more, and are influenced by other people and the world around them.

Within organizations, there have been traditionally two ways of looking at problem situations. One way has been looking at problem people, the other has been looking at problem events.[17] In the problem-people approach, a problem can be solved only if the difficult person is changed or removed. In the problem-event approach there is a specific problem to be solved and if everyone gets together it can be solved with a particular plan of action. Many management schools and consultants favor this approach and seek to put a problem-solving program in place. Both centering prayer and natural systems theory take a different approach. Understanding comes from thinking about and working with a whole process, not just a single person or event.

Christian mystical tradition has long considered a person's relationship with God to be not a static thing but rather a process. First, there is the process of the life journey. Athanasius's *Life of Antony* provides a look at that process. In the first step, Antony wants to be converted. He gives up his current lifestyle; then, exhausted from the change, he turns to Christ. He does good works and finally in some sense becomes Christ. This process is called *theopoiesis* or being made divine.[18] Second, within centering prayer there is the process of the prayer itself and the effect the prayer has on the individual. Keating writes about our relationship with God as being a developmental process. In a chapter about *Lectio Divina*, or the reading of the scriptures, Keating draws on the medieval monastic understanding of the "four senses of Scripture."[19] That is, there are four levels of reading the Scripture: literal, moral, allegorical, and unitive.

When the scripture is read for the literal sense, it is read to find out what is happening and who is involved. When the same passage is read in the moral sense, it is read for values and ways of behaving. In the allegorical sense, the passages are read to develop a life of practice for the reader. When the passages are read in the unitive sense no action is required; rather there is a sense of resting in God, a oneness between God and the reader. During this reading process, a relationship is being developed with God. In the first stage, there is an acquaintanceship with God; in the second, there is more of a friendliness; in the third, a friendship develops; and finally there is union of life.[20] Centering prayer is a process of interior transformation. This process of drawing closer to God and learning through unknowing is the subject of a poem by St. John of the Cross, "Entreme donde no supe."

I came into the unknown
and stayed there unknowing,
rising above all science.
I did not know the door
but when I found the way,
unknowing where I was,
I learned enormous things,
but what I felt I cannot say,
for I remained unknowing,
rising beyond all science.[21]

Natural systems theory is also based on and works through process. In defining process, Michael Kerr says that process is a continuous series of actions that result in a given set of circumstances or phenomena. Content, he writes, is taking those results out of the context of those actions. Edwin Friedman applies this understanding of "process" and "content," to churches and congregations. Friedman writes, "Efforts to bring about change by dealing only with symptoms (content), rather than process, never will achieve lasting changes in an organic system."[22] The distinction that is drawn here is important for congregational change. Just as process is important for individual change through centering prayer, so too is it important in focusing on change in the congregation. Process is emotional and about relationships. Content is about specific events and is usually a symptom of a problem in a relationship. What that means is that if you solve one content problem, another content problem will arise to replace it until the underlying process or relationship issues are finally addressed.

A bishop in the Episcopal Church used to ask his congregational leaders why one priest could move altar candlesticks an inch and be fired, and another priest could move the church building across town and be given a raise. The answer to that question was that the issue was not about buildings or candlesticks, but rather was about relationship systems within the congregation. There are always content issues in a congregation; they can be about budget, theology, minister, members, guilds, or groups. Unless the relationship process is the focus, the content will continue to revolve from issue to issue.

The Role of the Emotions, Family of Origin, and Automatic Functioning

The impact of the emotions on human functioning, the role of the family of origin in the development and response of these emotions, and the impact of these emotions on a person's ability to function are important concepts in both centering prayer and natural systems theory. Both centering prayer and natural systems theory see human emotions as a natural part of human existence, but a part of human existence that can easily dominate human behavior and lead to a reduction in thought-based decisions and a concomitant increase in automatic emotional functioning.

Emotions

Among the modern writers on the subject of prayer, Thomas Keating has the most developed understanding of the role the emotions play in a person's spiritual development. Keating writes, "Emotions faithfully respond to what our value system is."[23] Because of that, emotions are our best friends along the spiritual journey. While we can lie to ourselves about what is important to us, the emotions faithfully record what our true values are. Whenever our conscious or unconscious desires are frustrated, our emotional response begins without any thought on our part. With each emotion there is a running commentary of wrongs done to us in the past, and those wrongs that might be done to us in the future. This commentary heightens a person's feelings and intensifies a person's response. This interaction between emotions and commentary is a process that is very hard to stop and often controls the way a person functions.

In natural systems theory, unlike centering prayer, emotions are not thought of as a description of a feeling or state such as anger, apathy, or lust; rather, they refer to a subjective experience of the emotional system. In a family, it describes the relationships among father, mother, and children; in an organization it describes the relationship among the members of that organization. "*Emotional* refers to all the systems that guide an individual automatically within an environment. These are instinctual behaviors that guide an individual."[24] These behaviors may include, but not be limited to, facial expressions and feelings—like falling in love, illness, migration, sex. The emotional system is shaped by the person and the person is shaped by the system.

The Family and Emotion

Centering prayer and natural systems theory each see the family of origin as having a primary role in the emotional process. The relationship the person has within his or her family continues on throughout their whole life. The way that a person functions within that family of origin is the way that they will continue to function throughout their lives.

Thomas Keating, writing about this process, describes it as emotional programs for happiness.[25] As infants, we have various wants and desires that remain unmet. Infants are, by nature, helpless, and their needs, both material and emotional, are met by others, often their parents or siblings. The primary caregiver holds, kisses, and hugs the infant, communicating love and affection. This gives the infant a feeling of security. But there is always a time in even the most cherished infant's life when the primary caregiver is not available. As the infant becomes a toddler, she or he begins to compete with other family members for the time and recognition of the primary caregivers.

When the child moves out into the wider community, there is more competition, and often the child is frustrated in satisfying his or her basic needs. Later in life, we may not remember the actual events, but the emotional results of these events remain with us. For children who have suffered emotional trauma in the early part of their lives, the effects on the later part of their lives are that much more dramatic. The child may mature intellectually and physically, but emotionally they still react in ways that were developed in infancy.

We have an unlimited capacity for more: more power, more control, more affection, and more esteem. Within each of us, says Keating, there are emotional energy centers in which reside desires for power, control, affection, and esteem. The rejections, from our childhoods both real and imagined, are carried forward into the present. These are not rational centers and don't require thought;

they are emotional reactions on the subconscious level. Try as we might, we are unable to control them. So, instead, we replay our childhood reactions in our adulthood with disastrous results. This set of reactions is translated into emotional programs for happiness that can't work because we are no longer children and we, as adults, can't meet those needs for power, control, affection, and esteem that we had as children.[26]

A child, for example, may have never been chosen first to be on an athletic team on the playground. In fact, this child may have always been chosen last. As a result, as an adult they always strive to be chosen. They don't really want the job, the award, the spouse, they want to be chosen. When not chosen, they react with anger or sadness. These unconscious emotional programs for happiness are visible on the conscious level. As we have seen, they were catalogued as early as the fourth century, by Evagrius Ponticus, as gluttony, impurity, avarice, sadness, anger, restlessness, vainglory, or pride.[27] These drives and desires, when in place, often cause us to function automatically, without thought and in response to relationships that we had in our family of origin.

Murray Bowen writes that the molecule of the family system is the triangle. The triangle is the smallest stable relationship system and the triangle has relationship patterns that repeat in times of stress. The original triangle is father, mother, and child.[28] The way a child functions, the role the child plays, and the child's position in the family of origin are often the way the child will function later in life. Michael Kerr writes that

> *The existence of a family emotional field is the product of an emotionally driven relationship process that is present in all families....This emotional process results in people occupying different functioning positions in the family. A person's functioning position has a*

significant influence on his beliefs, values, attitudes, feelings, and behavior.[29]

This process of transmission of role, function, and behaviors is not only generational but multigenerational. This is more than the past influencing the present, it is the past being present in the present. The result of all of this is that people are less free to make thoughtful decisions than might be supposed.

The Automatic Process

Centering prayer and natural systems theory apologists see much of human functioning as unconscious and programmed. The area in our lives in which we make thought-based decisions is relatively small. Instead, we are driven by forces and processes outside our selves. Early Christian mystics such as Evagrius Ponticus described these as demons and wrote in terms of temptations. This was language that was appropriate to its time in describing the human internal process. Modern Christian writers speak in terms of programs for happiness developed in childhood that are carried into adulthood. These programs represent values that, while they may be appropriate for a two-year old struggling with life, are not appropriate for an adult. These values are represented by uncontrolled desires for more affection, power, control, and esteem. This, in some sense, is the nature of sin. The emotions that these Christian writers describe are more limited in scope than the emotional processes that the systems theorists describe. The natural systems theorists would call feelings what the Christian writers describe as emotions. The systems theorists' emotional field or system is a much broader concept, including not only feelings, but also other biological functions and processes.

Anxiety, say natural systems theorists, leads people to respond automatically to a perceived threat. The response may be based on the emotions, not on the reality of the threat. People who are more differentiated from the emotional systems around them will be aware of their own emotions and their response to the threat. The less differentiated person is more likely to react automatically in ways that are not appropriate to the reality of the threat.[30]

In either case, the result is to limit rational decision-making and functioning. One of the goals for both the centering prayer practitioner and the natural systems theorist is to increase thought-based decisions and decrease automatic functioning through the limiting of emotional reactivity and the development of an independent self.

The Self and the Projection Processes

Murray Bowen writes that parents often project their problems onto a child. In a family, a single child may be the focus or it may be more than one child. This is a process that is universal to all families and its purpose is to lessen anxiety. In recent times this has been called "scapegoating." This process can also be found in congregations which single out a clergy or member as being the cause of all their problems. If the person or persons are removed, then the system will find a replacement for the person removed and no overall change will take place. Thomas Keating also writes of projection. People will project onto others the responsibility for their happiness or unhappiness. People will project onto God their own needs for control, affection, power, and esteem. But both centering prayer and natural systems theory place responsibility on the self and not on beings outside the self.

In both centering prayer and natural systems theory the concept of self plays a central role. The self, says Thomas Keating, is made in the likeness of God with the ability to love unconditionally, create, nurture, and strengthen as is appropriate to a being created in God's likeness. But humans develop a self instead, that is made in its own likeness, one that is based on a person's needs for affection, esteem, power, and control. Keating calls this self a false self.[31]

The false self is built upon our desires for material goods and success, sometimes at the expense of others. This gives us a sense of self based on what we have, what and who we control, and what other people think and say about us. This can also include identification with other groups and organizations to the point that we believe our worth is bound with the goals and success of the group. Benignly, it could be a sports team or a school; less benignly the National Socialist Party in pre-World War II Germany. The false self is the self that we set up that tells us we need to satisfy the energy centers through a program for happiness that involves acquiring symbols of worth. These symbols enhance our self-image in our own eyes. We thus communicate to ourselves: "I am a worthy person because I have a new house or a big car," or "I feel good when the USC football team wins because that means I am a winner."

The true self is one that needs only to be in relationship with God and whose purpose is to love unconditionally. It is for this purpose that humankind was created.

The concept of differentiation of self is at the core of natural systems theory, writes Daniel V. Papero.[32] This refers to the amount of differentiation between intellectual and emotional functioning.[33] On one end are people who are dominated in their intellectual and emotional functioning by the automatic emotional process of the family system. These people are less flexible and less adaptable in times of stress. This leads to greater reactivity and anxiety. At the other end are people who can function intellectually more independently from the family system and in times of stress are more adaptable and less reactive to anxiety. This independence allows them rational choices. This is not to make a value judgment on their worth in a community. It is only an acknowledgment of the way in which they function. Each bring to the community their own level of functioning and whatever gifts they may have to offer in terms of personal skills and talents.

Within natural systems theory, the self is made up of clearly defined beliefs, opinions, convictions, and principles.[34] This self is unchangeable. It is made up of all the conscious decisions and choices made from birth based on experience and reason. Natural systems theory also puts forth the concept of the pseudo-self. The pseudo-self is acquired, conforms to the environment, and is created by the emotional pressure of the group. The pseudo-self can borrow self from others to enhance its well-being. Joining groups and identifying with other people are ways for this process to take place. A person who is continually in the process of self-differentiating is more able to make rational thought-based decisions, and less likely to be swept up in the reactivity of the moment. These people know who they are and are comfortable with diversity because they don't need to appropriate self from a group, organization, or thing to feel whole.

A key in both centering prayer and natural systems theory is that the individual is responsible for him- or herself. In natural systems theory, the understanding is that you cannot change the behavior of others, but you can change your reaction to that behavior. By changing your own reaction, you then impact the system around you. The change in your reactions will necessitate change in the actions of others.

In centering prayer, one of the recognized fruits of the prayer is unconditional acceptance of others. Centering prayer changes the life of persons who pray, enabling them to act in the present without regard to what Thomas Keating calls the afflictive emotions and the commentary that builds these emotions to a fever pitch.

Both centering prayer and natural systems theory seek to nurture and bring out a self that can act freely and independently of the pressures within the systems of which they are a part. In both of these understandings, it is a life-long and continuing process rather than a thing achieved in a moment and possessed from that moment on. In both of these systems a person becomes a "true self" or a "differentiated self" through gaining the ability to act consciously and independently while still being connected to others through relationship.

Physiology

It has long been known that the body and mind act upon each other. A major theme in both theology and philosophy, beginning with the Greeks, has been the struggle between the mind and body. They have, at times, been portrayed as being at war with each other. The mind is generally given the role of controlling the desires of the body. The body is given the role of leading the mind astray along the path of concupiscence. Balance between the two needs to be maintained. Peter Brown writes, "An unaffected symbiosis of body and soul was the aim both of medicine and philosophical exhortation."[35] Another way of viewing the mind and body is as a relationship with each acting and influencing the other. Instead of being separate or in a hierarchy, they are parts of a whole.

Centering prayer and natural systems theory both adhere to the understanding that there is a close relationship between the mind and the body. In the history of Christian mysticism, physiological effects have long been recorded. The histories of the desert fathers and mothers and the *Life of Antony* all record physiological changes that take place during prayer. Evagrius Ponticus writes about the effects of anger on the body. Anger leads to indignation and "this is succeeded by a general debility of the body, malnutrition with its attendant pallor and the illusions of being attacked by poisonous wild beasts."[36]

These effects need to be noted or observed and opposed with prayer. Evagrius writes, "when you grow angry...then is the time to put yourself in mind of prayer....You will find that the disordered movement will immediately be stilled."[37] The author of *The Cloud of Unknowing* also writes of this relationship, "for it is God's will to be served in both body and soul together as is seemly, and to give man his reward, in bliss, both in body and soul."[38] The benefits of *apatheia*, achieved in prayer and stressed by early Christian writers from Clement to Cassian, include mental relief from stress and anxiety but also physical relief.

The body–mind connection is also noted by writers of natural systems theory. Physiology is part of the greater relationship system, writes Louise Rauseo. In her article, "Relationships as Primary Regulators of Physiology," she maintains that social relationships and physiology are related and are important in understanding a person's life course. Heart rate, blood pressure, and other physical factors have long been known to be affected by the reactivity among people.[39] Disease is often found where there are troubled human relationships. Rauseo says, "Physiology is as sensitively tuned to the 'charge' of important relationships as it is to external life-threatening dangers. Information about relationships is often pre-verbal and may bring about responses before a thought is formed."[40] Instability in the emotional or family system can lead to physical changes. These can include heart attack, asthma, colitis, and perhaps even depression and varicose veins. People with higher levels of differentiation are not as affected as those people who have lower levels of differentiation and are therefore more reactive to the relationship system.

If the natural systems theory understanding of physiology and relationship systems is valid and the Christian mystic's understanding of the effects of prayer is also correct, then centering prayer could be used as a way of counteracting the physiological symptoms of relationship. Prayer could be a method of directly moderating anxiety and its physical effects. Centering prayer might be a way of lowering the overall reactivity of the relationship system in a congregation.

Implications for Congregational Leadership

The first implication for leadership is that congregational systems need to be understood as mutuality or reciprocity. In this way of thinking, A does not cause B so much as A and B influence each other. In the congregation all the people who make up that body, lay and ordained, leader and follower, regular attender and occasional visitor, and their families and generations of families, all mutually influence each other. Congregational leadership looks at the relationship that all of these different people, parts, and events have with each other and how they function in relation as part of one another. The leader constantly monitors and works with these relationship systems. Centering prayer helps us to experience ourselves as part of the greater whole of God. It helps us to feel and be in relationship with God and God's creation.

The second implication is that leadership is best achieved through the process of self-differentiation. Leaders need to take responsibility for themselves, their actions and their responsibilities in the system. Leaders need to define their own objectives and goals and work toward them while staying in touch with other parts of the congregation.[41] Most importantly, they need to stay in touch with those parts of the congregation that are opposed to or working actively against their goals and objectives. Leaders also need to be as non-reactive as possible. The centering prayer goal of *apatheia* becomes a necessity in congregational leadership. This can only be achieved with an active centering prayer practice on the part of both lay and ordained leaders. Those leaders, in turn, need to be supported by active centering prayer groups within the congregation. Active centering prayer lowers the overall reactivity of both the individuals and the congregation as a whole. Centering prayer also works to slow down or interrupt the physiological effects of increased reactivity and anxiety. Natural systems theory can help us understand the emotional field that is a congregation and the position of the leader in that system. But theory needs the complement of centering prayer to work effectively within that system and maintain the non-reactive leadership position.

The third implication is that all people in the congregational system need to observe their own behavior and position within the system and objectively see the ways that they function within the system. The more objective people are, the more able they are to see the role that they play in whatever the current issue is and not blame others. The answer to any question is always "me," because both centering prayer and natural systems theory teach that the only person one can affect is "me." Michael Kerr writes, "If one does not see himself as part of the system, his only options are either to try to get others to change or withdraw."[42] If, on the other hand, one accepts responsibility for one's position in the system and remains objective about the position one plays, then the amount of reactivity will decrease. The purgative process of centering prayer allows one to act in the present in a more objective and less reactive manner.

The last implication for congregational leadership is that reactivity and anxiety can only be reduced in an open congregational system. Murray Bowen writes, "Relative openness does not increase the level of differentiation in a family, but it reduces anxiety, and a continued low level of anxiety permits motivated family members to begin slow steps toward better differentiation."[43] Centering prayer begins a process of openness though its purgation of past hurts and an opening of a greater relationship with God. This experience of a loving relationship with God provides a model of being loved unconditionally. This personal experience of being loved unconditionally provides the example and the security one needs to love other people unconditionally. This, in turn, leads to a willingness to risk being open with others.

Centering prayer and natural systems theory are companions in the process of congregational leadership. Centering prayer makes possible the self-differentiation that natural systems theory requires. The personal healing of centering prayer leads to the possibility of congregational healing as the spiritual health of the individual, in a systems view, affects relationships throughout the whole system.

Notes

Chapter One—Introduction

1. Ellen Hill, "Resurrection: Renewal and Rebirth in Congregations Which Have Experienced Betrayal of the Pastoral Trust," D.Min. project, Claremont School of Theology, 1997 (Ann Arbor, MI: UMI, 1997), 53.
2. Ibid., 50.
3. Conversation with the Reverend Canon D. Bruce MacPherson, Canon to the Ordinary, Diocese of Los Angeles, 1992.
4. G. Lloyd Rediger, *Clergy Killers: Guidance for Pastors and Congregations Under Attack* (Inver Grove Heights, MN: Logos Productions, 1997), 6–7.
5. Edwin H. Friedman, *Generation to Generation: Family Process in Church and Synagogue* (New York: Guilford Press, 1985).
6. Tiglath-pileser III (745–727 B.C.E.) was the founder of the Assyrian Empire of this era. He was an able ruler who developed the policy of resettlement for those who rebelled against him instead of brutal reprisals.
7. Kathleen Dale and Paul Lawson, "12 Things to Remember." Paper presented at The Conference of Diocesan Executives, Seattle, WA, April 1996.
8. Michael E. Kerr and Murray Bowen, *Family Evaluation* (New York: W.W. Norton, 1988), 24.
9. Ibid., 23.
10. Peter Steinke, *How Your Church Family Works* (Washington, DC: Alban Institute, 1993), 3.
11. M. Basil Pennington, *Centering Prayer* (Garden City, NY: Image Books, 1980), 61.
12. *The Cloud of Unknowing*, ed. James Walsh (New York: Paulist Press, 1981), 135.
13. Pennington, 62.
14. Thelma Hall, *Too Deep for Words: Rediscovering Lectio Divina* (New York: Paulist Press, 1988), 36–41.
15. Thomas Keating, *Intimacy with God* (New York: Crossroad, 1995), 12.

Chapter 2
1. Such causes include differing styles of leadership, liturgical preference, and styles of management. The individual content of these issues might vary along congregational or denominational lines. Sermons might be too liberal or too conservative, management too tight or too loose, or churchship too high or too low.
2. Harry Harrison, *The Death World Trilogy* (New York: Berkeley Medallion Books, 1960), 133.
3. G. Lloyd Rediger, "Clergy Killers," **Leaven** 13, no. 7 (May 1994): 1.
4. Ibid., 1.
5. Ibid.
6. Kerr and Bowen, 112–14.
7. Edwin H. Friedman, "Bowen Theory and Therapy," in *Handbook of Family Therapy*, vol. 2, Alan S. Gurman and David P. Kniskern, eds. (New York: Brunner/Mazel, 1991), 140.
8. Kerr and Bowen, 113.
9. The Cranberries, "Zombies," "No Need to Argue," Island Records, 1994.
10. Friedman, *Generation to Generation*, 202.
11. Ibid., 206.
12. James E. Jones, "Chronic Anxiety: The Adrenocortical Response and Differentiation," **Family Systems** 1, no. 2 (Fall/Winter 1994): 134–35.
13. Friedman, *Generation to Generation*, 53.

Chapter 3
1. Margaret J. Wheatley, *Leadership and the New Science: Learning about Organization from an Orderly Universe* (San Francisco: Berrett-Koehler Publ., 1992), 6.
2. Ibid., 26.
3. John Tyler Bonner, "Differentiation in Cellular, Social and Family Systems," **Family Systems** 1, no. 1 (Spring/Summer 1994): 20.
4. Polly D. Caskie, "What Kind of System Is the Family?" **Family Systems** 1, no. 1 (Spring/Summer 1994): 14.
5. Friedman, "Bowen Theory and Therapy," 135.
6. Michael Kerr, "From the Editor." **Family Systems** 1, no. 1 (Spring/Summer 1994): 3.
7. Michael Kerr, "The Extension of Bowen Theory to Nonfamily Groups," in *The Emotional Side of Organizations*. Patricia Comella, ed. (Washington, DC: Georgetown Family Center, 1996), 15.
8. Ibid., 14.
9. Ibid., 10–13.
10. Ibid., 12.

11. Patricia Comella, "A Brief Summary of Bowen Family Systems Theory," in *The Emotional Side of Organizations*. Patricia Comella, ed. (Washington, DC: Georgetown Family Center, 1996), 5.

12. Dale and Lawson, "12 Things to Remember."

13. Jones, 138.

14. Ibid.

15. Steinke, *How Your Church Family Works*, 4.

16. Friedman, *Generation to Generation*, 15.

17. Ibid., 18.

18. Kerr and Bowen, 14.

19. Thomas Aquinas, *Summa Theologica*, trans. Fathers of the English Dominican Province (Westminster, MD: Christian Classics, 1948), Q3, Art. 6, Pt. 1.

20. Kerr and Bowen, 24.

21. Ibid., 10.

22. Ibid.

23. Caskie, 18.

24. Fritjof Capra, *The Turning Point* (New York: Bantam Books, 1983), 265.

25. Kerr and Bowen, 27.

26. Friedman, "Bowen Theory and Therapy," 145.

27. Kerr and Bowen, 28.

28. Peter L. Steinke, *Healthy Congregations: A Systems Approach* (Bethesda, MD: Alban Institute, 1996), 5.

29. Kathleen Dale, interview by author, 11 Dec. 1996.

30. Daniel Papero, *Bowen Family Systems Theory* (Boston: Allyn and Bacon, 1990), 43.

31. Kerr and Bowen, 59.

32. Ibid., 64–65.

33. Ibid., 61.

34. Friedman, "Bowen Theory and Therapy," 156.

35. Ibid.

36. Kerr and Bowen, 68.

37. Ibid., 95.

38. Friedman, "Bowen Theory and Therapy," 141.

39. Murray Bowen, *Family Therapy in Clinical Practice* (Northvale, NJ: Jason Aronson, 1985), 306.

40. Kerr and Bowen, 97.

41. Ibid., 100–07.

42. Papero, 47.

43. Friedman, *Generation to Generation*, 28.

44. Edward Schillebeeckx. *Ministry: Leadership in the Community of Jesus Christ* (New York: Crossroad, 1981), 31.

45. Ibid., 16.
46. Bowen, 306.
47. Friedman, "Bowen Theory and Therapy," 150.
48. Francis D. Andres, "An Introduction to Family Systems Theory," Georgetown Family Symposia 1 (1971–1972): 4.
49. Ibid., 5.
50. Bowen, 307.
51. Friedman, "Bowen Theory and Therapy," 151.
52. Ibid., 147.
53. Steinke, *How Your Church Family Works*, 34.
54. Edwin Friedman, interview by author, 22 April 1995.
55. Andres, 11.
56. Kerr and Bowen, 142.
57. Ibid., 271.
58. Ibid., 272.
59. Friedman, *Generation to Generation*, 229–30.
60. Ibid., 230.
61. Friedman interview.

Chapter 4
1. *The Episcopal Church: Essential Facts* (New York: Episcopal Church Center, 1980), 9.
2. *The Book of Common Prayer* (New York: Church Hymnal Corporation, 1979), 856.
3. Michael Casey, *Toward God: The Ancient Wisdom of Western Prayer* (Liguori, MO: Triumph Books, 1996), 174.
4. Thomas Keating, M. Basil Pennington, and Thomas Clarke, *Finding Grace at the Center* (Still River, MA: St. Bede Publications, 1978), 37–39.
5. Thomas Keating, interview by author, 21 Nov. 1986.
6. Keating, *Finding Grace at the Center*, 44.
7. Bernard McGinn, *The Foundations of Mysticism* (New York: Crossroad, 1991), 101.
8. Louis Bouyer, *The Spirituality of the New Testament and the Fathers*, vol. 1 of *A History of Christian Spirituality*, (New York: Seabury Press, 1963), 274–75.
9. Origen, "Against Celsus," [trans. Frederick Crombie], in *Fathers of the Third Century*, eds. Alexander Roberts and James Donaldson, vol. 4 of *Ante-Nicene Fathers* (Peabody, MA: Hendrickson, 1994), 475.
10. Bouyer, 299.
11. William A. Clebsch, preface to *The Life of Antony and the Letter to Marcellinus*, by Athanasius, trans. Robert C. Gregg (New York: Paulist Press, 1980), xiv.

12. Athanasius, *The Life of Antony and the Letter to Marcellinus*, trans. Robert C. Gregg (New York: Paulist Press, 1980), 42.
13. Owen Chadwick, *John Cassian*, 2d ed. (Cambridge: Cambridge University Press, 1968), 162.
14. Ibid., 107.
15. Philip Rousseau, *Ascetics, Authority, and the Church in the Age of Jerome and Cassian* (Oxford: Oxford University Press, 1978), 183.
16. Contemplative Service Resources, Centering Prayer, training manual for Contemplative Service Formation Retreat, Serra Retreat Center, Malibu, Calif., 23–25 Aug. 1996. The retreat was conducted by Contemplative Outreach of Southern California, Los Angeles, Appendix.
17. Keating, Pennington, and Clarke, 37.
18. Casey, 66.
19. Hall, 8.
20. Thomas Keating, *Open Mind, Open Heart: The Contemplative Dimension of the Gospel* (New York: Amity House, 1986), 21.
21. Pennington, 34.
22. Ibid., 27.
23. Gustave Reininger, "Centering Prayer and the Christian Contemplative Tradition," **Sewanee Theological Review** 40, no. 1 (Christmas 1996): 38.
24. Ibid., 38.
25. Keating, *Intimacy with God*, 32.
26. Pennington, 92.
27. Ibid., 61.
28. Ibid., 90.
29. Keating interview.
30. Pennington, 96.
31. Reininger, 36.
32. Thomas Keating, *Invitation to Love: The Way of Christian Contemplation* (Rockport, MA: Element, 1992), 40.
33. Keating, *Intimacy with God*, 163.
34. Keating, *Invitation to Love*, 12.
35. Evagrius Ponticus, *The Praktikos*, trans. John Bamberger (Kalamazoo, MI: Cistercian Publications, 1981), chap. 6, 16.
36. Keating, *Intimacy with God*, 72.
37. Tertullian, "The Soul's Testimony," [trans. S. Thelwall] in *Latin Christianity: Its Founder, Tertullian*, eds. Alexander Roberts and James Donaldson, vol. 3 of Ante-Nicene Fathers (Peabody, MA: Hendrickson, 1994), 177.
38. Keating, *Intimacy with God*, 165.
39. Ibid., 73.
40. Ibid., 76.

41. Reininger, 41.
42. Thomas Ward, "Centering Prayer: An Overview," **Sewanee Theological Review** 40, no. 1 (Christmas 1996): 24.
43. Contemplative Service Resources, *Centering Prayer*, 10.
44. Keating, *Intimacy with God*, 62.

Chapter 5
1. Bowen, 289.
2. Friedman, *Generation to Generation*, 195.
3. Kerr and Bowen, 80.
4. Daniel V. Papero, "Anxiety and Organizations," in *The Emotional Side of Organizations: Applications of Bowen Theory*, ed. Patricia A. Comella (Washington: Georgetown Family Center,1995), 47.
5. Ibid., 47–48.
6. Ibid., 49.
7. Keating, *Invitation to Love*, 8.
8. Keating, *Intimacy with God*, 72–75.
9. *Book of Common Prayer*, 351.
10. Hans Küng, *On Being a Christian* (Garden City, NY: Doubleday & Co., 1976), 75–77.
11. *Book of Common Prayer*, 370.
12. Sara Butler, "Pastoral Care and Centering Prayer," **Sewanee Theological Review** 40, no. 1(Christmas 1996): 58.
13. Keating, *Invitation to Love*, 87.
14. Steinke, *Healthy Congregations*, 3.
15. Edward O. Wilson, foreword to *The Sociobiology Debate: Readings on the Ethical and Scientific Issues Concerning Sociobiology*, ed. Arthur L. Caplan (New York: Harper & Row, 1978), xii.
16. Kerr and Bowen, 24.
17. George Parsons and Speed B. Leas, *Understanding Your Congregation as a System: The Manual* (Bethesda, MD: Alban Institute, 1993), 4–5.
18. Clebsch, xvi.
19. Keating, *Intimacy with God*, 46.
20. Contemplative Service Resources, Centering Prayer, 8–9.
21. John of the Cross, "I Came Into the Unknown," in *The Poems of John of the Cross*, trans. Willis Barnstone (New York: New Directions Book, 1972), 59, lines 1–10.
22. Friedman, *Generation to Generation*, 202.
23. Keating, *Invitation to Love*, 19.
24. Kathleen Dale, interview by author, 11 Dec. 1996.
25. Keating, *Invitation to Love*, 5.
26. Ibid., 8–13.

27. Evagrius Ponticus, 6–14.
28. Bowen, 198–201.
29. Kerr and Bowen, 55.
30. Jones, 127-41.
31. Keating, *Intimacy With God*, 163.
32. Papero, Bowen Family Systems Theory, 45.
33. Bowen, 363.
34. Ibid., 365.
35. Peter Brown, *The Body and Society: Men, Women, and Sexual Renunciation in Early Christianity* (New York: Columbia University Press, 1988), 27.
36. Evagrius Ponticus, *The Praktikos*, chap. 11, 18.
37. Evagrius Ponticus, *Chapters on Prayer*, chap. 12, 57.
38. *Cloud of Unknowing*, 212.
39. Louise Rauseo, "Relationships as Primary Regulators of Physiology," **Family Systems** 2, no. 2 (Fall\Winter 1995): 106.
40. Ibid., 113.
41. Friedman, *Generation to Generation*, 229.
42. Kerr and Bowen, 272.
43. Bowen, 537.

Bibliography

Books

Athanasius. *The Life of Antony and the Letter to Marcellinus*. Trans. Robert C. Gregg. New York: Paulist Press, 1980.

The Bible. Revised Standard Version.

The Book of Common Prayer. New York: Church Hymnal Corporation, 1979.

Bouyer, Louis. *The Spirituality of the New Testament and the Fathers*. Vol. 1 of *A History of Christian Spirituality*. New York: Seabury Press, 1963.

Bowen, Murray. *Family Therapy in Clinical Practice*. Northvale, NJ: Jason Aronson, 1985.

Brown, Peter. *The Body and Society: Men, Women, and Sexual Renunciation in Early Christianity*. New York: Columbia University Press, 1988.

Capra, Fritjof. *The Turning Point*. New York: Bantam Books, 1983.

Casey, Michael. *Toward God: The Ancient Wisdom of Western Prayer*. Liguori, MO: Triumph Books, 1996.

Chadwick, Owen. *John Cassian*. 2d ed. Cambridge: Cambridge University Press, 1968.

Clebsch, William A. Preface to *The Life of Antony and the Letter to Marcellinus*, by Athanasius. Trans. Robert C. Gregg. New York: Paulist Press, 1980.

Evagrius Ponticus. *The Praktikos and Chapters on Prayer*. Trans. John Bamberger. Kalamazoo Mich.: Cistercian Publications, 1981.

Friedman, Edwin H. *Generation to Generation: Family Process in Church and Synagogue*. New York: Guilford Press, 1985.

Hall, Thelma. *Too Deep for Words: Rediscovering Lectio Divina*. New York: Paulist Press, 1988.

Harrison, Harry. *The Death World Trilogy*. New York: Berkeley Medallion Books, 1960.

Jager, Willigis. *Contemplation: A Christian Path*. Liguori MO: Triumph Press, 1994.

117

John of the Cross. "I Came Into the Unknown." In *The Poems of John of the Cross.* Trans. Willis Barnstone. New York: New Directions Book, 1972.

Keating, Thomas. *Intimacy with God.* New York: Crossroad, 1995.

——. *Invitation to Love: The Way of Christian Contemplation.* New York: Continuum, 1995.

——. *Open Mind, Open Heart: The Contemplative Dimension of the Gospel.* New York: Continuum, 1995.

Keating, Thomas, M. Basil Pennington, and Thomas Clarke. *Finding Grace at the Center.* Still River, MA: St. Bede Publications, 1978.

Kerr, Michael E., and Murray Bowen. *Family Evaluation.* New York: W. W. Norton, 1988.

Kung, Hans. *On Being a Christian.* Garden City, NY: Doubleday & Co., 1976.

McGinn, Bernard. *The Foundations of Mysticism.* New York: Crossroad, 1991.

Origen. *Against Celsus.* [Trans. Frederick Crombie]. In *Fathers of the Third Century.* Eds. Alexander Roberts and James Donaldson. Vol. 4 of Ante-Nicene Fathers. Peabody, MA: Hendrickson, 1994.

Papero, Daniel V. *Bowen Family Systems Theory.* Boston: Allyn and Bacon, 1990.

Parsons, George, and Speed B. Leas. *Understanding Your Congregation as a System: The Manual.* Bethesda, MD: Alban Institute, 1993.

Pennington, Basil. *Centering Prayer: Renewing an Ancient Christian Prayer Form.* Garden City, NY: Image Books, 1980.

Rediger, G. Lloyd. *Clergy Killers: Guidance for Pastors and Congregations Under Attack.* Inver Grove Heights, MN: Logos Productions, 1997.

Rousseau, Philip. *Ascetics, Authority, and the Church in the Age of Jerome and Cassian.* Oxford: Oxford University Press, 1978.

Schillebeeckx, Edward. *Ministry: Leadership in the Community of Jesus Christ.* New York: Crossroad, 1981.

Steinke, Peter L. Healthy Congregations: A Systems Approach. Bethesda, MD: Alban Institute, 1996.

——. *How Your Church Family Works: Understanding Congregations as Emotional Systems.* Washington, DC: Alban Institute, 1993.

Tertullian. *The Soul's Testimony.* [Trans. S. Thelwall]. In *Latin Christianity: Its Founder, Tertullian.* Eds. Alexander Roberts and James Donaldson. Vol. 3 of Ante-Nicene Fathers. Peabody, MA: Hendrickson, 1994.

Thomas Aquinas. *Summa Theologica.* Trans. by Fathers of the English Dominican Province. Westminster, MD: Christian Classics, 1948.

Wheatley, Margaret J. *Leadership and the New Science: Learning about Organization from an Orderly Universe.* San Francisco: Berrett-Koehler, 1992.

Wilson, Edward O. Foreword to *The Sociobiology Debate: Readings on the Ethical and Scientific Issues Concerning Sociobiology.* Ed. Arthur L. Caplan. New York: Harper & Row, 1978.

Articles

Andres, Francis D. "An Introduction to Family Systems Theory." **Georgetown Family Symposia** 1 (1971–1972): 1–13.

Bonner, John Tyler. "Differentiation in Cellular, Social and Family Systems." **Family Systems** 1, no. 1 (Spring/Summer1994): 20–32.

Butler, Sara. "Pastoral Care and Centering Payer." **Sewanee Theological Review** 40, no. 1 (Christmas 1996): 55–61.

Caskie, Polly D. "What Kind of System Is the Family?" **Family Systems** 1, no. 1 (Spring/Summer 1994): 7–19.

Comella, Patricia. "A Brief Summary of Bowen Family Systems Theory." In *The Emotional Side of Organizations.* Ed. Patricia Comella, 5–7. Washington DC: Georgetown Family Center, 1996.

Friedman, Edwin H. "Bowen Theory and Therapy." In *Handbook of Family Therapy.* Vol. 2. Eds. Alan S. Gurman and David P. Kniskern, 134–70. New York: Brunner/Mazel, 1991.

Jones, James E. "Chronic Anxiety, the Adrenocortical Response, and Differentiation." **Family Systems** 1, no. 2 (Fall/Winter 1994): 127–41.

Kerr, Michael. "The Extension of Bowen Theory to Nonfamily Groups." In *The Emotional Side of Organizations.* Ed. Patricia Comella, 8–17. Washington DC: Georgetown Family Center, 1996.

———. "From the Editor." **Family Systems** 1, no. 1 (Spring/Summer 1994): 2–6.

Papero, Daniel V. "Anxiety and Organizations." In *The Emotional Side of Organizations: Applications of Bowen Theory.* Ed. Patricia A. Comella, 47–53. Washington, DC: Georgetown Family Center, 1995.

Rauseo, Louise. "Relationships as Primary Regulators of Physiology." *Family Systems* 2, no. 2 (Fall/Winter 1995): 101–15.

Rediger, G. Lloyd. "Clergy Killers." **Leaven** 13, no.7 (May 1994): 1.

Reininger, Gustave. "Centering Prayer and the Christian Contemplative Tradition." **Sewanee Theological Review** 40, no. 1 (Christmas 1996): 29–45.

Walsh, James, ed. *The Cloud of Unknowing.* New York: Paulist Press, 1981.

Ward, Thomas. "Centering Prayer: An Overview." **Sewanee Theological Review** 40, no. 1 (Christmas 1996): 18–28.

Other Sources

Contemplative Service Resources. *Centering Prayer.* Training manual for Contemplative Service Formation Retreat. Serra Retreat Center, Malibu, Calif. 23–25 Aug. 1996.

The Cranberries. "Zombie." *No Need to Argue.* Island Records, 1994.

Dale, Kathleen. Interview by author. 11 Dec.1996.

Dale, Kathleen, and Paul Lawson. "12 Things to Remember." Paper presented at The Conference of Diocesan Executives of the Episcopal Church. Seattle, WA., April 1996.

The Episcopal Church: Essential Facts. New York: Episcopal Church Center, 1980.

Friedman, Edwin. Interview by author. 22 April 1995.

Hill, Ellen. *Resurrection: Renewal and Rebirth in Congregations Which Have Experienced Betrayal of the Pastoral Trust.* D.Min. project, Claremont School of Theology, 1997. Ann Arbor, UMI, 1997. 97-32814.

Keating, Thomas. Interview by author. 21 Nov. 1986.